When Child Abuse Comes to Church

When Child Abuse Comes to Church

Recognizing Its Occurrence
and What to Do About it

Bill Anderson

BETHANY HOUSE PUBLISHERS
MINNEAPOLIS, MINNESOTA 55438

All names in this book have been changed, and some situations have been modified to protect the privacy of people involved in this story.

Unless otherwise noted, the Scripture quotations in this publication are from the New King James Version of the Bible, copyright © 1979, 1980, 1982, Thomas Nelson Inc., Publishers.

Scripture quotations marked NIV are taken from the Holy Bible, New International Version. Copyright © 1973, 1978, 1984 International Bible Society. Used by permission of Zondervan Bible Publishers. All rights reserved.

Published by Bethany House Publishers
A Ministry of Bethany Fellowship, Inc.
6820 Auto Club Road, Minneapolis, Minnesota 55438

Printed in the United States of America

Library of Congress Cataloging-in-Publication Data

Anderson, Bill, 1946–
   When child abuse comes to church / Bill Anderson.
      p.   cm.
   Includes bibliographical references.

   1. Sexually abused children—Pastoral counseling of.
2. Christian education of children—Case studies.
3. Child molesting—Prevention—Case studies.
4. Child molesting—Religious aspects—Christianity.
I. Title.
BV4464.3.A53   1992
261.8'32—dc20   92–30228
ISBN 1–55661–286–9   CIP

To all the children whose stories are represented
in this book in the hope that others will be
spared from suffering as they did.

BILL ANDERSON was the senior pastor of churches in Ohio and Pennsylvania for fifteen years, then the development officer for Baptist Bible College of Pennsylvania for two years, and is presently serving as senior pastor of a church in Michigan. He is a graduate of Bob Jones University (B.A.) and Faith Theological Seminary (M.Div.). He and his wife have three children.

Contents

Child Sexual Abuse

An Unavoidable Subject

The sexual abuse of children is becoming a tragic epidemic in our country. Although hard numbers are difficult to come by, these are the estimates: one out of three girls and one out of five boys will experience some form of sexual abuse by age eighteen. This translates into upward of thirty-eight million victims throughout the various racial, cultural, and socioeconomic strata of our society.

What this means for churches is that none can expect to remain unaffected by the problem. Just as the church cannot successfully insulate itself from other societal ills, such as the skyrocketing divorce rate or the spread of AIDS, it cannot avoid having to deal at some level or other with child sexual abuse.

As I travel and speak on this subject, I am often asked if the increase is in actual cases of abuse or just in our awareness of it. Although authorities hesitate to be dogmatic about this, it is my perception that both are true. Why am I so sure no church is immune? Here are the facts.

Between 1976 and 1984 the reporting of child sexual abuse rose two hundred percent. The federal Child Abuse Prevention and Treatment Act of 1974 established The National Center on Child Abuse and Neglect (NCCAN) to coordinate federal funding of research and treatment programs. Since then, all fifty states have passed child protection laws that require professionals such as doctors, teachers, and child-care providers to report suspected cases of child abuse.

Between 1984 and 1990 certain shocking cases of child sexual abuse caught the nation's attention and reporting again rose dramatically. These cases, such as Jordan in Minnesota and McMartin in California, were spectacular because they involved multiple perpetrators charged with abusing large numbers of children. In the McMartin case, indictments were first handed down in March 1984 against seven workers in a day-care center in Manhattan Beach, California. Eventually, they were charged with 354 counts of criminal sexual conduct, but in January 1986 charges against all but two of the defendants were dropped. In July 1987, the remaining two defendants, charged with abusing 14 children, were finally brought to trial. The trial dragged on until January 1990 when the defendants were acquitted. Because of the prolonged news coverage in this case alone, the general public became sensitized to the subject of child sexual abuse.

In addition to increased reporting, though, the crime itself appears to be on the rise. As more and more women enter the work force, there is an ever-increasing need for child care outside the home. This along with such things as the breakup of the nuclear family, the increase of single or divorced mothers, and the rise in the number of blended families resulting from remarriage may give abusers access to a larger number of potential victims. There also may be a cyclical effect in that more abuse creates more abusers. Many perpetrators were themselves abused as children. It is possible that as the number of victims rises, the number of abusers rises exponentially.

Additionally, the bombardment of sexual over-stimulation in movies, on television, and in advertising mirrors a culture that, despite all its strides toward equal rights for women, still views women (and young girls) as depersonalized objects for the sexual gratification of men. Sexually irresponsible sports figures and entertainers are held up as role models. Sex is portrayed as something that can be divorced from personal responsibility and self-control.

In the midst of this cultural milieu, with all its dangers and pitfalls, the church of Jesus Christ is called to service.

The purpose of this book is to alert the Christian community to the growing problem of child sexual abuse and to educate pastors, church leaders, and parents about the issues and dynamics involved. Ignorance spells danger. Education is the first line of defense in protecting our children.

From powerful experience, I know this is so.

Most churches will never encounter the magnitude of sexual abuse that we did. That is not to say, however, that we are the only church to ever have high numbers of sexual abuse victims. But because we experienced something of a microcosm of child sexual abuse, our story includes almost all of the related problems, only a few of which would have to be dealt with in most situations. In fact, most church leaders could serve a lifetime and never deal with the entire gamut of issues that arose in our church in a period of months. We had to struggle our way through practical, legal, medical, and theological issues. Among the many questions that arose were:

How could we have prevented the abuse?

How could we have detected it earlier?

What should we do when we learn of it?

What are the needs of child victims?

What kind of help do perpetrators need and who should help them? What should we do when the perpetrator is also a member of the church?

Where can we find help? Should we seek help from community-based social service agencies and secular counselors?

What is the best way to deal with the news media, the police, the courts?

What are the theological implications in such areas as legal proceedings, church discipline, and forgiveness?

These questions and many more demanded solid answers. And sometimes we had very little time to find them. A crisis situation does not lend

12

itself to clear thinking. It is my hope that our story will prepare others to deal wisely with child sexual abuse—either by dealing systematically and effectively with abuse that has occurred or, better yet, by taking preventive measures to keep it from occurring.

ONE

Crisis

A Framework for Making Critical Decisions

What would you do if you discovered that sexual abuse was taking place right in your church? Or in a church family? Suppose you learned or suspected that someone in your church—an elder, youth worker, Sunday-school teacher, or nursery worker—had a clouded history of sexually abusing children?

If you think it can't happen in your church, think again.

Sexual abuse involving children is a tangled and painful path to walk through, as churches across our land are finding out. First comes a shocking discovery, followed by the difficulty of sorting through accusations, confronting (or even *finding*) the perpetrator, seeking help for the victims, notifying the right legal authorities. The steps seem endless and confusing. Add to them the shock waves that come from the community-at-large and the congregation. A Christian leader is left to wonder how he can hold together a church family, let alone his own emotional well-being.

In this book, I will do more than retell our own story of struggle, and I only relate the incidents as they happened to us because I believe that experience is a valuable teacher. But more than that, of course, I intend to relate the best help, compiled both from experience and experts, that can help you walk through the wave after wave of trauma that results when sexual abuse comes to church.

How well I recall the day when I felt I was about to be overwhelmed.

It was late Saturday night and I was alone in my office—trying to relax and think. Although I didn't know exactly what the next morning would bring, this looked like the calm before the storm. The previous sixteen months had been difficult enough, but now I would have to face the news media. This was new territory for me—in over twenty years of ministry I had never had to deal with reporters.

I savored the quiet. Moments like this would be rare after tomorrow morning's front page headlines. Needing to build up some reserves of inner stamina for what was to come, I quietly prayed for spiritual strength and for wisdom from above.

I thought back to midmorning on Friday when our receptionist had buzzed me to say Julie Muldoon was on the line. Julie, an assistant prosecuting attorney, had been in touch with me several times recently, so I wasn't surprised to receive a call from her. But her strained tone of voice alerted me that this call was different from the others. She got right to the point. "Reverend, I've got bad news. A reporter from the *Times* was just here. He knows about the sexual abuse, but I don't think he knows the name of your church yet. I'll keep you posted if I get any further word."

The day I had dreaded for so long had arrived! A reporter from our local newspaper had finally caught wind of the staggering case of sexual abuse in our church—a case that had consumed a large part of my life since I became pastor of the church nearly a year and a half earlier. At least sixty-four children had been molested and physically abused. For a year or more prior to my coming, boys and girls had been raped, sodomized, beaten, and forced to participate in oral sex. The abuse had actually occurred in various parts of the church building, as well as on our school playground, and in the children's own homes and yards.

The police investigators, the juvenile court workers, and the prosecutor's staff had hoped this case would not catch the interest of the newspeople. It had been the most difficult case they'd ever faced, and news headlines would only complicate it. For me, and certainly for the families involved, the tragedy had caused months of anguish, uncertainty, fear, and anger. Sensational media attention would only intensify these painful emotions.

Our county's Sex Abuse Task Force, made up of representatives from several social service agencies, had warned me to expect national media attention because of the extent of the abuse. But for some unexplained reason, even though everyone had been dealing with it openly, the papers had not gotten hold of it. With wise foresight, however, the Task Force and Judge McCoy of the juvenile court had developed a strategy for dealing with the newspeople if and when the story broke. Our deacons and I also had discussed various ways to handle the situation when the news came out. Essentially I wanted to be as open as possible while protecting the privacy of the victims and their families.

Julie Muldoon called back about noon. "Reverend, I hate to have to tell you, but the reporter has talked to the judge and he already knew the name of your church. He's probably going to want to interview you next."

It was time to put our plan into action. I called Gary Cranston, editor of the *Times*. We had gotten acquainted months earlier and I knew he was a Christian. I would talk to the reporter later, but I wanted to go to the top first. I believed Cranston would be sympathetic when he learned what we had already gone through.

When I reached Cranston I told him I had a problem I'd like to discuss.

"I know," he said. "Our city editor sent me a note this morning, saying I ought to check out a story in our computer. I just read it. I've got time right now if you want to talk about it."

Over the next half hour I told him the whole story and how we had handled it each step along the way. My first concern was to convince him we were not covering up a scandal and that there had been no negligence on our part—in a sense, the

18

church itself had been victimized. I wanted him to feel the pain of our families and to sense the damage he could inflict if he handled the story carelessly.

We discussed the issue several more times on Friday and again on Saturday. Early Saturday I talked to the chairman of our deacons to decide how to handle the Sunday morning service. Should we broadcast live on the radio as usual? Should I change my text and deal with the news story in the message?

We had been making periodic reports to the congregation for over a year, so the news would not shock them. We saw no need to change the sermon. I would continue the series I had begun several weeks before. Also, because we had nothing to hide, we decided to do the live broadcast. After all, nothing was new except the news coverage itself.

This was a big story for a small paper—one that would certainly boost sales above its usual 53,000-copy Sunday circulation. Cranston and several of his editors worked overtime Saturday on the final draft. They even consulted the publisher, whose office was in another city, about the details of the story and the timing of its release. I asked Cranston to hold it until Monday so it wouldn't disrupt our worship on Sunday. What difference could one more day make? After all, the story was nearly two years old already.

Late Saturday he called to say the decision had been made. The story would run Sunday—on the front page. Worse, it would go out over the Associated Press wire late Saturday night and be statewide by Sunday morning. This, he explained, would insure that no other paper would scoop them. What it also insured was that all television news departments would be alerted in time to get crews to us by Sunday. I asked for an advance copy of the article so I could at least get a head start on preparing for questions it would generate. In a rare bending of the paper's policy, Cranston hand-delivered a computer printout to my office about 7:30 P.M. Saturday.

I was glad I had it early. Seeing it all in print was a real jolt. Normally the names of juvenile perpetrators are kept confidential; but in this case they not only named one convicted perpetrator, they also named his older brother, who had been implicated and charged but not yet brought to trial.

Alone in my office, I read the article twice. The case had involved an incredible series of events. What an ordeal this had been for the church, the families involved, and for me.

I was concerned about keeping straight the enormous number of details when the press interviewed me, and I was glad I had followed advice to keep a journal. It had been a useful tool several times during the protracted police investigation. I turned to it again—this time to review the sequence of main events for the inevitable interviews to come. I didn't expect reporters to call ahead for appointments, and I wanted to be prepared for spur-of-the-moment, on-camera questions. Everyone had suffered enough, and I didn't want to add to the misery by saying foolish things to the press.

The Advantage of Hindsight

Two years have now elapsed since our story was reported and nearly four years since the abuse occurred. We have had time to reflect on the events and our handling of them. Also, because of our high visibility, I have had the opportunity to talk with dozens of ministry leaders who have had to deal with some form of sexual abuse. Although we didn't handle everything well, we learned from our mistakes as well as our successes. In detailing both throughout this book, I hope to clear a path through the minefield of child sexual abuse that others can follow to safety.

When You Are the Key

The person in charge has an unenviable position when a crisis occurs. Like it or not, the pastor plays a critical role when child sexual abuse is suspected in the church or in a church family. The steps he takes will have far-reaching ramifications, either for good or bad, in the life of individuals, families, the church, and the community. This is a tremendous weight of responsibility, especially when decisions must be made quickly and with little or no prior experience in sexual abuse situations.

When you are the key to a painful situation well handled or badly handled, it is important to decide from the start how you will manage it: the right beginning will determine the best outcome.

Unfortunately, some ministry leaders opt for

"solutions" that are at best not helpful and at worst dangerous, unethical, or illegal. There is an integrity crisis of tremendous proportions in the Christian world, and, sad to say, some pastors are the worst examples.

Many in the ministry have been subverted into believing that a flawless image must be maintained at all costs. The substance of spirituality has become less important than the illusion of success, and anything that threatens to mar the image must therefore be concealed from public view. A pastor overcome by this kind of worldliness will be far less interested in protecting his flock than in protecting his own reputation. Engaging in damage control, sweeping the problem under the rug, and hushing it up may be the pastor's way of dealing with sexual abuse. In this kind of spiritually unhealthy atmosphere, the abuser may actually be shielded or excused through some form of convoluted mental gymnastics, while the victim may be blamed or discredited. Those who would try to intervene to solve the problem may find themselves blasted with "righteous anger" or have some sort of sanctions placed against them. It's hard to believe, I know, but such things do happen in "good, Bible-believing" churches.

A less pernicious but equally dangerous response is to simply ignore the problem. Some leaders lack the fortitude needed to face a problem squarely and deal with it. One danger of hushing up or ignoring an incident of child sexual abuse is that rarely does a perpetrator have only one victim. It is not uncommon for an adult-fixated offender to have 50 or more victims before being caught, and one study reported that a group of pedophiles had confessed to having an average of 380 victims each. By suppressing or ignoring available information, a pastor permits a perpetrator to have continued access to victims.

Confidentiality and accountability are two concerns for a pastor, and there is sometimes a tension between the two. There are few, if any, circumstances when an issue that is potentially dangerous or harmful to innocent people should be held in *absolute confidence* by a pastor. There may be legal ramifications to this statement, however, so pastors should be aware of "breach of confidentiality" and "invasion of privacy" laws in their state.

Nonetheless, a pastor who knowingly lets a church remain at risk commits a serious breach of pastoral responsibility. A genuine shepherd protects the sheep; only a hireling leaves the flock exposed to danger.

Even pastors with benevolent intentions may have attitudes or preconceived ideas that hinder them from making wise choices. Although they may not actually voice it, some have an *it-can't-happen-here* mentality that prevents them from taking precautions against sexual abuse. Subconsciously we all believe that bad things happen to other people in other places. But this sort of head-in-the-sand approach is not only dangerous but inexcusable in light of the information available to us.

Well-meaning pastors may also be at a disadvantage when dealing with habitual offenders.

Having been trained to forgive and to think the best of people, they may be too quick to accept a shallow repentance or a promise of "I won't ever do it again." Treating an offense too lightly or failing to deal thoroughly with an offender can leave the door open for further abuse.

Looking back on twenty-three years of pastoral ministry, I recall two cases of incest when I did exactly that. Although I treated them as seriously and thoroughly as I knew how at the time, I would treat them much differently today, given the knowledge I now possess. Pastors with limited experience or expertise should not rely on their own kind instincts when dealing with sex offenders who may be in the grip of life-dominating, addictive behavior.

Perhaps the most helpful attitude a pastor can adopt is to admit that he doesn't know it all.

The single most important decision I made was to find people who had experience in dealing with sexual abuse cases and to call upon them for help. I began this search the first day I learned of the possibility of abuse. It took only a few weeks to build a network of people, both in Christian ministries and in community social service organizations, who could help. These contacts enabled our church to avoid some serious mistakes and provide much better care for our people.

Early in the process I got acquainted with staff members of a large church that had experienced a case strikingly similar to ours a few years earlier. Simpson Community Church was located within an hour's drive of us, and I called on them repeatedly. The pastoral staff gave me invaluable guidance in mapping out an overall strategy and answering tough questions as they arose.

The apostle Paul said to the Ephesian elders, "Take heed to yourselves and to all the flock, among which the Holy Spirit has made you overseers" (Acts 20:28). As this verse suggests, taking care of yourself is prerequisite to taking care of the flock. Pastors, especially those in high-stress situations, should pay attention to their own mental, emotional, spiritual, and physical health. Finding someone who will give you sound spiritual advice, and making a commitment beforehand that you will follow it, is crucial to your ability to function well.

When I came to the church, I sought out an accountability partner. In a nearby city I found a seasoned pastor whom I held in high regard, and he agreed to meet with me monthly. When the abuse was uncovered, he made time for me whenever I needed to talk. This was extremely important when the number of details and my own emotional involvement threatened to cloud my judgment.

Four years ago I knew very little about child sexual abuse, and I have been disturbed to learn what a large problem it is in our culture. The head of our local Council on Child Abuse and Neglect calls it "pandemic." As a result, many resources and agencies are available to help deal with it. I was pleased to find a number of Christian men and women working in secular organizations in our area. Church leaders would do well to acquaint themselves with the social services—both secular and Christian—available in their community before the need arises to call for their help.

Two Kinds of Abuse

Although this book is primarily about child sexual abuse, the story is closely related to another kind of abuse that is being recognized more and more in churches and Christian ministries. For a long time we had no name for it. We could only catalog its characteristics and observe its devastating effects. But David Johnson and Jeff Van-Vonderen have described this phenomenon in a book called *The Subtle Power of Spiritual Abuse,* which finally gives a name to a dangerous style of leadership that is all too common in churches and religious organizations.[1] They use the term "spiritual abuse" because people in leadership positions can wrongly use their authority to exert control over others in ways that parallel emotional, physical, or sexual abuse. As in other kinds of abuse, a perpetrator uses power to victimize weaker people. And, as in other kinds of abuse, the victims suffer tremendous trauma and often need outside intervention to survive the ordeal.

In *Churches That Abuse,* Ronald Enroth describes ten identifying characteristics of spiritually abusive churches: control-oriented leader-

---

[1] To keep this writing focused on the problem of the physical and sexual abuse of children, I must limit the discussion of wrong attitudes among church leaders. But I highly recommend that Christian leaders read both books mentioned in this chapter: *The Subtle Power of Spiritual Abuse* by David Johnson and Jeff VanVonderen and *Churches That Abuse* by Ronald Enroth.

ship, spiritual elitism ("we're better than others"), manipulation of members (through guilt, fear, and intimidation), perceived persecution (paranoia), life-style rigidity (legalism), emphasis on experience (subjective emotionalism), suppression of dissent, harsh discipline of members, denunciation of other churches, and the painful exit process.

A main concern, described in both books, is that abusive leaders deny problems and refuse to let members of their congregations talk out conflicts. The result is a sick atmosphere in which all manner of problems is compounded.

Shortly after I became pastor of the church, I began to recognize the symptoms that something was wrong. At the time, I didn't see them as part of a larger, more complex problem. But I now realize that our story of sexual abuse is incomplete without acknowledging the role spiritual abuse played in it. Because of the way problems were typically denied and swept under the rug, our church was especially vulnerable to sexual abuse. Though never spoken, there was an underlying implication that it was better to leave dangerous people on the loose than to deal properly with them and thus jeopardize the image of perfection that had been so carefully cultivated.

In addition to making the church a place where sexual abuse could easily go unnoticed, the spiritual abuse had residual effects that made the healing process for sexual abuse victims much more difficult to manage.

This does not mean that child sexual abuse happens only in churches where spiritual abuse is a problem or that a church which experiences sexual abuse is of necessity spiritually abusive. Sexual abuse can and does happen in all kinds of churches. But in a spiritually abusive atmosphere the danger of widespread sexual abuse is greater, and the difficulty of dealing with it increases dramatically.

———————

The main point is this: When a child is victimized and the abuse has occurred in your church family, it is urgent that the leaders choose the right attitude as they are called upon to handle the problem. No doubt, this will be one of the most painful situations you will ever face in your life; but as servants of Christ, we need to know how to help and heal hurting little ones who are in our care.

And that's why I recommend that a spiritual leader involve himself as much as possible in the events in and around child sexual abuse—even from the outset, when it's necessary to investigate charges as they first come to light.

And so we will turn our attention, first, to the beginning of this difficult path—that is, to the need for full, wise investigation.

TWO

Investigation

What to Do When You Suspect Abuse

For me, this story began shortly after I arrived as pastor of this midsized congregation in a mostly blue-collar community in 1988. About 350 people were attending Sunday morning worship services when I came on the scene, but attendance had peaked at over 500 a few years earlier. The church had a 50-year history in its "rurban" community of about 1,000 people.

I accepted the position specifically because I was intrigued by the critical problems the church faced and because of the challenge they posed. Each of my three previous pastorates had been in a troubled church, and I had come to see myself as a sort of turn-around specialist. My initial evaluation was that it would be a big job to bring this ministry back to health, but I felt compelled by the Holy Spirit to give it a try.

It took only a couple of weeks on the job to see that I had seriously underestimated the situation.

I knew about the financial problems, and I knew the congregation was polarized over some unresolved conflicts. I also knew there had been a big drop in attendance over the previous two years. What I didn't know about was the abuse of power that accounted for these problems.

In my third week, while trying to bring some order out of the chaos, I got a particularly unsettling phone call from one of our young fathers. Bob wanted to know if I could stop by his house to talk with him and his wife, Darla. He explained his urgency. Their two-year-old son, Ricky, had been sexually molested, and it looked as if it had happened at church.

I agreed to stop by that evening as soon as they got the children to bed.

As I sat sipping tea at their dining room table late that night, I could hardly believe the story they recounted to me. And I couldn't imagine the trauma of everything they had already been through.

In the second week of August, Ricky had been running a slight fever, so they stopped at a Med Center on their way home from church to have him checked. What they assumed would be a routine physical examination of their son became instead a horrifying investigation of their whole family. The doctor on duty informed them he had found physical and behavioral evidence of sexual abuse and referred them to their family pediatrician. The following day the pediatrician confirmed the diagnosis and, in accord with state law, reported it to Child Protective Services. In the ensuing investigation the agency treated Bob not only as a *potential* suspect but as the *prime* suspect.

Reporting Sexual Abuse

What constitutes sexual abuse varies by definition from state to state as do the penalties for criminal sexual conduct. The National Center on Child Abuse and Neglect (NCCAN) defines child sexual abuse as "contacts or interactions between a child and an adult when the child is being used for the sexual stimulation of that adult or another person." The difficulty with this and all definitions is that the terms have to be defined. For instance, people from birth through age eighteen are generally considered children. However, the age of consent varies widely from state to state, ranging from fourteen to eighteen years of age. Adolescents and children can also be perpetrators, and an age spread of five years between the victim and the perpetrator is sometimes used as a guideline for determining abuse.

In addition to physical acts—such as genital or oral stimulation, fondling, digital penetration, and anal or vaginal intercourse—child sexual abuse may include nonphysical acts such as indecent exposure (exhibitionism), obscene phone calls, peeping toms (voyeurism), permitting children to view adults engaging in sex acts (primal scene), and filming or photographing children for pornographic purposes.

Since 1974 each of the fifty states has enacted "reporting laws" concerning suspected child abuse and neglect. Do you know what the law in your state requires of you?

In our state, for example, the Child Protection Law specifically lists sexual abuse and sexual exploitation as criminal behavior and requires health-care professionals, teachers, counselors, and others to report suspected cases to Child Protective Services. This agency falls under the County and State Departments of Social Services and is responsible for promptly investigating reported instances of abuse. When the safety of the child is in question, this agency has the right to temporarily remove the child from the home. If evidence of abuse is found, they report their findings to a law enforcement agency for a criminal investigation. Our state's penal code defines criminal sexual conduct in the first, second, third, and fourth degree. First through third degree are felonies, and first degree, being the most serious, carries a maximum sentence of life imprisonment for adult offenders. The crimes are defined the same for juvenile offenders, but the punishment differs. Instead of a prison sentence, juveniles are ordered into various kinds of treatment programs and can usually be kept only until a certain maximum age. The law was recently revised so that juvenile offenders can be kept in rehabilitation to age twenty-one instead of age nineteen as it was previously.

Why is it important for you, as a church and community leader, to know such laws?

Those required to report suspected abuse may be fined for not doing so and are protected from civil litigation that may arise from their report.

You do not need *proof* of abuse, only the *suspicion* of it, to be required to report it. Usually, a report made by phone must be followed in a certain number of days with a written report giving specific information.

Pastors are not required in every state to report suspected abuse, but it is the ethical thing to do since child sexual abuse is criminal behavior. One exception in reporting may be when the information comes to the pastor as a confession in a counseling situation. Some states protect the confidentiality of information from this "priest-penitent" relationship, and legal advice should be sought in such circumstances. To find what reporting laws exist in your state, call your county Department of Social Services, juvenile court, or any agency dealing with child protection.

After two weeks, Child Protective Services ruled out abuse by Bob and Darla, relatives, or baby-sitters and dropped the case. They were interested only in abuse in the home by primary care-givers.

Bob explained that the circumstantial evidence turned up during their investigation pointed at the church as the most likely place the abuse had occurred. He also mentioned two other families who thought their children might have been molested at church.

When I checked with those two families, neither was concerned enough to press the issue. The evidence, they said, was too circumstantial and they were willing to ignore it. At that point, I had no reason to argue with them.

I couldn't imagine how such a thing could happen in our church. I knew, however, that it was too risky to deny the possibility that it had. My three immediate problems were: how to ensure that no further abuse occurred; how to investigate without driving the perpetrator undercover, only to emerge later, unsuspected; and deciding whom I could trust to help me with the first two.

I had never had to play detective before, and I began to wish my seminary training had included a couple of FBI courses. I knew I needed help in handling this, but I really had only one contact in the community, a friend from college days who had agreed to be my accountability partner.

Due to his own lack of experience with anything like this, he couldn't give me specific advice. But he did give me the names of several local professionals who could give me direction.

Networking from my friend's list added a whole new dimension to my education. I spent hours every day for weeks talking to social service people and reading books and pamphlets.

If you have never had specific training about child sexual abuse, it is important for you to come up-to-speed quickly, and with the best information.

Investigation

The investigation of child sexual abuse is itself a difficult process. Parents, church leaders, child protection workers, therapists, and prosecutors each have an interest in the facts of a case; but their interests are not always the same and may at times be at cross purposes to one another. To facilitate healing, for example, a therapist may use certain techniques in questioning a child, but those techniques might later be used to have the case thrown out of court.

Professionals should be called upon to investigate the facts. If the case results in a criminal trial, it is extremely important that the prosecution not be jeopardized by a well-intentioned but bungled investigation.

Pastors and parents of victims should resist the inclination to conduct an investigation on their own unless there is no possibility of leaving this to trained professionals. For instance, an American missionary may be confronted with a case of sexual abuse in a foreign country where the laws are lax or the police are more corrupt than the criminals. In such a case, there may be no other recourse than to interview the victim and confront the alleged perpetrator.

Another reason to use professionals has to do with the emotionalism that surrounds child sexual abuse. Since the matter is so repugnant, it is difficult for those with some personal interest in the case to evaluate the evidence objectively. A trained professional will come at the investigation in a more detached way and thus avoid complicating the issue with emotionally clouded judgment. By nature, investigations create strained relationships, even those conducted in a professional and responsible way. The strain is multiplied when the investigation is attempted by those with a high emotional stake in the matter.

By urging the use of professionals, I am not suggesting that parents should not be active participants in investigations involving their children. Parents, when possible, should see that investigators are skilled with children. As in any other profession, some are better than others. Before I urged Ricky's parents to make a police report, I checked with experienced people to see if there were law enforcement officers in our area who were specifically trained to deal with children. Our county sheriff's department and state police post both had staff members trained in this area. So, before Bob made his police report, he was assured that he would be dealing with someone who was skilled with and sensitive toward children.

The adults who are responsible should also concern themselves about the number and nature of the interviews their children are subjected to. It is possible to victimize children a second time by the stress of the investigation. For instance, it may be necessary for a Child Protection worker to initially interview the child. If evidence of abuse is found, it is likely that a law enforcement officer will want to question the child. It may then be important to find a therapist who will also want to hear the story repeated. If the case goes to court, a prosecutor will want to gather information from the child about the incident, and later the defense attorney will have the right to an interrogation in preparation for the trial. The child may then be required to testify in court as well. All together, the victim may be asked to repeat the story a dozen or more times. If possible, avoid the necessity of multiple interviews by gathering several interested parties together to hear the child's testimony on a single occasion, thus relieving the victim of any more stress than is absolutely necessary.

I'd been on the job less than a month when this came to light, and I had no idea whom I could trust. For all I knew, the perpetrator could be someone in charge of a children's ministry.

Finally I confided in the person I'd been in contact with during the interview process: the chairman of the official board. He was the one I knew the best. After hearing the story, he recommended that we involve two other people—the Sunday school superintendent and head usher—to keep an eye on the halls, rest rooms, nurseries, and classrooms during public services. We hoped this would turn up some clues without tipping our hand.

Several questions confronted us at this point. Were other children involved? What kind of symptoms should we be looking for in them? What does a perpetrator look like? How would we recognize one? How could an offender gain access to our children during church? Why hadn't anybody become suspicious of anything? Had we been negligent?

All we knew was that Ricky became highly agitated when his parents tried to leave him in the nursery, and he made vague claims that his teacher had hurt him. This was of little help in zeroing in on the perpetrator, because volunteers in that nursery rotated, and Ricky was unable to identify the teacher. Nor would he say exactly how he had been hurt.

We started looking for symptoms in other children from that nursery. We asked parents if their sons or daughters had shown any abrupt or marked changes of behavior or if they had developed any unexplained physical problems. To my horror, I learned that several had developed serious fears of the nursery and at least two had suspicious physical symptoms.

Symptoms

Signs of child sexual abuse can be detected by an alert parent or child-care worker, and this information should be incorporated in the training of all children's workers in the church and in a parents' seminar on the subject, which every church should conduct annually.

The first clue in our case came from the doctor's physical exam. In taking Ricky's temperature rectally, the doctor found redness and swelling of the anal area. He also noted Ricky's unusual behavior during the exam. A two-year-old would be a little uncomfortable during this procedure, but Ricky objected far too violently, indicating the possibility that he had been hurt in this way before.

Another abused child, however, may show the opposite behavioral symptoms. In 1962 pediatrician Dr. C. Henry Kempe coined the term "battered child syndrome" to describe a child who doesn't cry when injected with a needle, doesn't object to being separated from parents, and lies perfectly still when being dressed or undressed. This too is abnormal behavior learned in an abusive situation. Children know they cannot withstand the attacks of adults who are always smarter and more powerful, so the only form of defense they know is acquiescence.

In all cases, the thing to note is behavior that is abnormal in some way. Each child, depending on age and circumstances, is likely to show signs of abuse differently and, especially in the early stages, the symptoms may be passed over by those who care for the child. It is also possible that any one symptom by itself could be explained by something other than abuse, but symptoms clustered together should be seen as a definite warning signal.

The kinds of physical symptoms one should be alert to are:

- redness or swelling in the anal area
- vaginal or rectal bleeding, pain, itching, or swollen genitals
- pain in urinating or defecating
- unusual odors in the genital area
- vaginal infections, discharge, or venereal disease
- pregnancy in a child
- torn, stained, or bloody underclothing
- unexplained persistent sore throat or gagging (due to oral sex)
- difficulty in walking or sitting
- physical complaints with no apparent somatic base

Behavioral symptoms could include:

- extreme changes in behavior such as sudden loss/increase in appetite
- a sudden refusal to do something previously enjoyed or be with someone previously liked
- recurrent nightmares or disturbed sleep patterns and fear of the dark
- regression to more infantile behavior such as bed-wetting, soiling underclothing, thumb-sucking, or excessive crying
- unusual interest in or knowledge of sexual matters, expressing affection in ways inappropriate for a child of that age, or acting in an unusually seductive way with peers or adults
- unusual sexual themes expressed through the child's schoolwork, art, poems, stories
- fear of a person or an intense dislike at being left somewhere or with someone
- aggressive, disruptive, or self-abusive behavior
- withdrawal, running away, or failure in school
- an unwillingness to undress or to participate in physical education classes
- expression by the child that he/she has been involved sexually with an older person

Along with his sudden fear of the nursery, Ricky also began having terrible nightmares. They became so disruptive that Bob had to sleep in another part of the house just to get enough rest to function on his job. Still, it wasn't until the doctor's findings that the picture of abuse came clearly into focus. The cluster of both behavioral and physical symptoms forced Bob and Darla to conclude that Ricky had been abused.

It is often difficult to understand how symptoms of abuse can go unrecognized for what they are. But more often than not they do. In one church where several children had been abused in the nursery, the parents would meet at the nursery door with their screaming children. In embarrassment they would say to one another, "I don't know what has gotten into my child. He never acts this way at home." They didn't know how to explain the unusual behavior, and they were embarrassed to be thought of as poor disciplinarians. The children's fears were a signal of abuse, but such a thing never entered the parents' minds.

Physical symptoms of abuse are not always interpreted properly even by those in the medical profession. One little girl in our nursery had a bladder infection that puzzled her doctor for months because he had never seen it in anyone other than sexually active women. Yet the possibility of sexual abuse did not occur to him. One little boy had recurrent bleeding from the rectum. His doctor attributed it to constipation, although he admitted it was a strange case. Later, when the doctor learned the boy had been repeatedly sodomized, he was extremely embarrassed that he had been so blind.

There is also the possibility that some victims will show no outward signs of abuse. This was true of 43 percent of the children in one study. Still, adults should be on the alert for strange or unexplained physical or behavioral changes in children under their care.

We started watching our nursery-aged children in other settings to see if they feared a particular individual. We checked the nursery records for any clues or irregularities. And we started monitoring the movement of people during our services and programs.

False Accusations

One of the men on patrol noticed that on several occasions a young, childless couple left the auditorium about ten minutes into a worship service and went to the nursery for the remainder of the time. Nursery attendance was taken during the first part of the hour, so by going in late they were able to spend a lot of time in the nursery without showing up on the workers roster. Not only did this look suspicious, it was strictly against our policy. Only assigned workers or their substitutes were to be in the nurseries. This had been simply ignored. In addition, we learned that some of the children were afraid of this man. When meeting him in the halls they would cling to their parent's legs or hide behind them. We began to think we had our perpetrator.

Only narrowly did we escape making a serious mistake. Circumstantial evidence pointed toward this fellow, but he was innocent. He and his wife simply considered the services dull and preferred to care for children. We also learned that some of the older children had been frightening the younger ones with scary stories about this man, so their fear of him could be explained. We were glad we had moved cautiously and made no hasty accusations. We could have seriously damaged the reputation of an innocent person.

The fact that we came close to accusing an innocent man again raises the issue of the need to act with integrity in dealing with alleged abuse. This is a highly charged, emotional subject, and accusations should not be made without careful consideration. If a child accuses an individual, however, the child should be taken seriously. Experts believe that children, especially very young children, almost never lie about sexual abuse. If the accused person is a paid staff member, insurance companies recommend that he or she be suspended with pay while a quiet investigation is conducted. In the absence of a definite accusation by a victim, circumstantial evidence should be treated especially carefully.

For nearly four weeks after my first meeting with Bob and Darla, nothing of any consequence turned up. We couldn't imagine who the offender might be or how he was operating. But then we got a breakthrough, and it came through Ricky.

Due to Ricky's extreme fear, Bob and Darla had not put him in the nursery for months. But when he regained his emotional equilibrium at home, his parents decided to take him to the nursery again to see how he'd do.

As soon as Ricky was confronted by Donald, an eleven-year-old boy, the little child became hysterical. He claimed that Donald had hurt him. After further questioning by his mother, Ricky revealed that Donald had hurt the toddler's bottom. Bob relayed this new information to me on Sunday afternoon, and that evening I called our deacons together. For the first time, I told the entire group all I knew, and we began a series of private prayer meetings to ask God for wisdom.

I began to hear of other children who were afraid of Donald. A little checking revealed that he came from an extremely troubled home. The parents were in divorce proceedings, and the father no longer lived with the family. He had been arrested for indecent exposure, and his wife, Cynthia, had openly accused him of abusing her and of having hard-core pornography in the house. She also had hinted that he had molested his own children.

Then I learned that Donald not only worked often in our nurseries but that he and his older brother and sister regularly baby-sat free of charge for many of our young families. This answered the question of access. To my dismay, I realized that nearly every young child in our congregation had been available to him.

Once we had some pieces of the puzzle, we had to figure out where they fit.

When I spoke to the pastor of Simpson Community Church, he was amazed that Child Protective Services had not already referred the case to the police for a criminal investigation.

"I really think you should tell what you know to the state police," he advised, and he gave me the name of the officer who had handled their case.

I encouraged Ricky's parents to make a police report, but Bob, remembering the trauma of the initial investigation, was reluctant to submit himself to that possibility a second time. To allay his fears, I had him come to my office while I called the state trooper and explained Bob's concerns. The officer assured me that Bob would not be treated as a suspect, then logged my call and referred the report to our local state police post. The next day an officer, Sgt. Ault, interviewed me and made an appointment to talk with Ricky and his parents.

During the interview in their home I sat quietly in the corner. I was there strictly for moral support. The officer's ability with children was immediately apparent. Within fifteen minutes he had Ricky demonstrating on a doll what had been done to him. Bob and Darla watched in silence as their little boy revealed things that parents hope their children will never experience. In the following months I would witness this pain again and again with parent after parent.

As tragic as this was, after so many weeks of uncertainty and frustration, it was, in a sense, a relief to finally have a definite accusation.

Armed with this information from Ricky, Sgt. Ault interviewed Donald at school five days later with a school counselor and caseworker from Child Protective Services present. Donald denied everything, but the officer believed the boy was lying. Sgt. Ault advised us, however, that without a confession it would be useless to press charges.

Ricky was too young to testify in court, he said, so there would be no chance of getting a conviction.

It was difficult for me to believe, knowing what we did, that we should simply drop the matter.

About noon that same day the youth pastor from a nearby church called. "Bill, can you come to my office right away?" he pleaded. "Donald's mother is on her way over here with Donald right now, and I'd like you to be here."

Shaken by the police interview, Donald had gone straight home and told his mother about it. His mother, who had never met me, immediately called the youth pastor at the church she'd been attending with her parents.

When I arrived, Cynthia, a slightly built, attractive woman in her late thirties, was already in the office. Though obviously distraught and struggling to keep her composure, she was extremely cooperative. The three of us discussed the case for a few minutes and then called Donald into the room. This was my first introduction to the boy, and I was surprised by how small and shy he was. I was expecting some big, tough, bully type. Although he was eleven, he looked no more than eight, and he certainly didn't appear to be much of a threat to anybody. Looking at him, I couldn't help but wonder if we were making a terrible mistake.

Perpetrators

Most of the images people have of sex offenders are inaccurate stereotypes. The fact is, there is very little, if anything, in appearance that would mark a person as a child molester. Even so, there seems to be a mentality that says, "I would know a sex offender if I saw one."

A suspect in another case started attending a church nearby and began working in their nursery.

When a parent who was aware of the situation called the pastor to warn him he was taking an unwarranted risk, the pastor responded coolly, "I haven't seen any behavior of that kind, so I see no reason to restrict the person from working with our children."

Taken aback by his attitude, the mother asked, "Just exactly what would you look for in a child molester?"

The pastor admitted he didn't know, but he was sure this person didn't fit the description. His misconception was that nice-looking people don't do this sort of thing.

One persistent myth is that of the "dirty old man," a stranger who lurks in parks to prey upon unsuspecting children. The standard warning parents give their children to not take candy or accept favors from strangers is insufficient. In reality, 95 percent of sexually abused children are victimized by a family member or by some person they know and trust. In one study, half of all abusers were under age thirty-one; only ten percent were over age fifty.

It was difficult to believe that Donald was a child molester. He had a small, frail appearance and was actually a child himself. He was a quiet, well-mannered boy who had grown up in the church. Many of the women remembered his baby shower. Everyone knew him and liked him. Even more, everyone trusted him.

A pleasing personality is a common characteristic of a sex offender. They are often regarded as quiet, nice people. In addition, they frequently come from dysfunctional, destructive home environments where substance abuse is prevalent. They may live without a positive male role model or with an abusive male in the home. Molesting other children becomes a way of gaining power or control that is otherwise lacking in their lives.

In *Helping Victims of Sexual Abuse,*[1] Lynn Heitritter and Jeanette Vought list the following categories of adolescent sex offenders:

The experimenter. A young person who in the course of exploring his developing sexuality takes advantage of children who are generally preschool age.

The loner. A young person who feels isolated from family and peers and abuses children to meet his emotional need for intimacy and self-esteem.

The boy next door. Typically an older teen who is socially well adjusted but self-centered and who abuses children for his own sexual gratification.

The aggressor. Typically the product of an abusive or disorganized home, this teen uses threats of force and violence in sex abuse. He can be seen as gregarious and charming by peers while having a history of antisocial behavior. He is motivated by a desire for domination, a need to express anger,

---

[1]Bethany House Publishers, 1989.

or a desire to humiliate his victims.

The group offender. This adolescent may not be abusive on his own but can be pressured by a group into committing sex abuse, especially if the group is led by one of the other types of sex offenders.

Adolescent female offenders. Usually in her early teens, this type of girl usually chooses children under age four and tends to stop after one or two acts of abuse.

Adults who prefer to have sex with children are called *pedophiles*, and textbooks list two types: "fixated" and "regressed." Fixated offenders have never progressed in their own psychosexual development past the level of relating to children. Regressed pedophiles, on the other hand, have experienced normal sexual relationships with adults but, due to some overwhelming stress in their lives, regress to desiring sex with children. Fixated offenders probably started abusing children as adolescents or earlier and are considered by experts to be the most dangerous type.

The three of us confronted Donald with the evidence, but he steadfastly denied everything. The best we could do was to get his mother to allow Sgt. Ault to interview him a second time.

A few days later the officer spent an hour with the mother and son in their home. Once more, he confronted Donald with Ricky's accusations. He explained to Donald that the way he sat and moved indicated he was lying. But Donald remained adamant in his denial and even agreed to take a polygraph test.

Before it could be scheduled, however, Donald's

mother's divorce attorney talked her out of allowing it.

Without a confession, and denied the one tool they could use to press for a confession, the police dropped the case. We were left holding the bag, one filled with a dangerous explosive, and I didn't know how to disarm it. If I pursued the investigation myself, it could blow up in my face. If I didn't, it would surely blow up in someone else's face—a child's. We already knew of at least one victim and thought there could be several more. But because they all were so young we couldn't prove a thing.

And so, two weeks after the initial police report and two months after we had started on this trail, we came to an impasse. If I didn't find a way to proceed, it was possible everything would be swept away, forgotten, denied.

Denial, as we will see in the following chapter, is one of the great hurdles you will face in any case of sexual abuse.

THREE

Denial

The Brick Wall Blocking Progress

Of all the difficulties associated with child sexual abuse, denial is perhaps the worst. Many times, even the victims do not want to acknowledge that it happened. In our case, the offender, his mother, the victims, their parents, the church leaders, the congregation, and even the newspeople were affected in one way or another by denial. I came to see it as a brick wall or, more accurately, as a series of brick walls laid parallel to one another. Just when we had gotten over or around one, we found our way blocked by yet another.

As long as people are in denial, other issues related to the abuse cannot be resolved. Denial prevents even the best efforts from having any therapeutic value.

The Dynamics of Denial

Denial is a psychological defense mechanism that comes into play when a person is faced with something too threatening or overwhelming to cope with. In its popular use the word covers a range of terms that include:[1]

Simple denial: to fail to acknowledge reality or tell the truth; dishonesty.

Minimization: to partially admit a problem in order to make it seem less serious or significant than it actually is.

Blame: to ascribe to someone or something other than self the responsibility for unacceptable behavior.

Rationalization: to offer inaccurate excuses to justify behavior.

Diversion: to change the subject to avoid dealing with something threatening or unpleasant.

Hostility: to become so angry at the mention of a subject that others hesitate to bring it up.

The dynamics of denial differ significantly from person to person, but they generally take one of two forms: lies or disbelief.

Lies

The people who lie about sexual abuse are making a conscious effort to cover the truth, but their motivation for lying is not always the same. The motives for denial on the part of perpetrators is fairly straightforward—they lie to avoid punishment.

One myth about sex abusers is that they are insane, but experts agree that a perpetrator who

---

[1]D. J. Anderson, *The Psychopathology of Denial* (Center City, Minnesota: Hazelden Foundation, 1981), pp. 11–12.

has lost touch with reality is the exception rather than the rule. They know what they are doing is wrong. That is why they go to such lengths to keep it secret. When caught, they almost always deny what they have done. When pushed further with the facts, they may fall into one of the other forms of denial. They may argue, "Yes, I did it, but I didn't hurt her" (minimization) or "The reason I did it was to teach her about sex" (rationalization) or "I wouldn't have done it if she hadn't seduced me" (blame).

Because denial is such a hindrance in therapy, most residential treatment programs will not admit adolescent offenders without a court order forcing an offender to stick with the program. Of those who enter voluntarily most drop out prematurely. This is why a conviction is so important. Without it most juvenile offenders have neither the will nor the finances to successfully complete treatment.

Victims also lie, but they do it out of fear. They generally do not lie about *who* abused them, or about *the kinds of things* that have been done to them. They simply deny the fact that they have been abused because they have been threatened and are extremely afraid. Unless a child has been thoroughly educated about sexual abuse and repeatedly conditioned to report any instance of it immediately, most will not.

Donald not only beat his victims and threatened them with death, he also threatened to kill their parents if they reported him. For children, whose security is wrapped up in their parents, nothing is more terrifying than the prospect of having them killed. By remaining silent the children felt they were protecting themselves and their parents as well.

These lies are opposite from the type people fear children will tell—that they will make up a story and ruin an innocent person's career, marriage, or reputation. Most experts agree that children rarely lie about this and that young children almost never do. It is not that they are incapable of lies and fantasies, but usually they are not malicious. Even children who have seen graphic sex on television would not be able to explain such things as how sperm tastes or what sex acts feel like. Usually false allegations by children are prompted by an adult who has a grudge against someone. Most of these instances involve fourteen- and fifteen-year-old girls, and even these are rare and usually easy to spot. A youngster who has been prompted will be unable to remain credible during repeated questioning by a doctor, child protection workers, police, and prosecutor.

Disbelief

As we became aware of more victims over a period of several months, I made periodic reports to the congregation during our midweek services. On three of these occasions one woman, with the same puzzled look on her face each time, raised her hand and asked, "But this didn't happen in our building, did it?" And each time I assured her that it had. She was experiencing denial born out of disbelief. It was impossible for her to imagine that so many horrendous acts had been committed in her church. It was overwhelming to think of children being raped, sodomized, forced into oral sex, beaten, and threatened right around the corner from where she was singing hymns and reading her Bible. There were many others like her, and their denial came in the form of disbelief. Even the newspeople showed symptoms of disbelief in some of their questions:

Question: Is a nine-year-old boy physically capable of rape and sodomy? *Answer:* Children have all the physical/sexual capabilities for arousal and orgasm. Kinsey, the noted sex researcher, found orgasms in male infants as young as five months.

Question: Could that many children be that brutalized and not tell their parents? *Answer:* In our case, not one child out of over sixty victims reported the abuse.

Question: Is it possible that dozens of nursery workers and parents could be so blind to something so widespread happening for so long? *Answer:* Denial in its different forms kept everyone from the truth for a very long time; such possibilities were so inconceivable it just never crossed anyone's mind.

Denial in parents is something of an automatic reflex that causes them to overlook or ignore warning signs. It's as if their minds cannot accept the possibility of such things happening to them or their children. It's not so much that they consciously reject the idea of abuse; it is more that the idea never reaches their consciousness. Many will later castigate themselves for being negligent; but denial, not negligence, is the real issue.

The police and Child Protective Services had failed to convince Donald to admit anything. Even his mother couldn't get him to confess. When she asked if he had hurt anybody, he flatly denied that he had. She wanted to believe him, and was torn between wanting to find the truth and fearing the consequences.

From the day of the first police interview, Donald expressed fear of being taken from his home. As time went on his mother shared that fear more and more. We knew of no leverage to get the case off dead center. Nobody could honestly bargain with him by promising that he would not be removed from his home if he confessed. The court reserves the right to make that decision based on such factors as the stability of the family, the number of offenses, and the level of coercion used in the abuse. If the perpetrator is seen as a continuing threat to the community, or if the court believes his family life would hinder therapy, the offender can be ordered into a long-term residential treatment program. If he is uncooperative in the treatment program, he may be sent to a Juvenile Detention Center, which is the equivalent of prison for adults.

It grieved me to think that Donald might slip through the cracks in the system and be doomed to a life of addictive behavior. But as it became clear that he might deny his guilt indefinitely, it became equally clear that we had a moral obligation to warn our families. We had not yet officially notified other parents of the possibility of abuse because Donald had not confessed, and dealing in unproved allegations made me ill at ease. But in mid-December 1988, I called all parents whose children were about the same age as Ricky and Maria, a little girl who also showed clear signs of sexual abuse. I told the parents about the two victims and warned them of the definite possibility of more. I disclosed that Donald was the prime suspect but that he had not yet confessed or been proven guilty. I also described physical and behavioral symptoms that they should look for in their children. The group voted to have a follow-up meeting the next week with the caseworker from Child Protective Services.

Several probable victims emerged from these meetings, but denial on the part of some parents became an immediate obstacle. They didn't want to acknowledge the clear evidence, and it didn't take much to get them to dismiss it altogether. Many went home and asked their children if anything had happened to them. When their children said no (and they all said no), the parents simply dropped the issue. In some cases it was a year before they were forced to admit that their children had indeed been victimized. Others followed up with medical exams, but for most there was no physical evidence so many months after the fact. Still, a negative exam from the family doctor was all the fuel some needed to keep the fires of denial burning.

Dealing with parents in denial is delicate work. The confrontational aspect cannot be avoided. The pastor is in the awkward position of trying to convince parents of something they don't want to know but need to acknowledge for the good of their children. If the pastor tries too hard to push emotionally strung-out parents through denial, he risks becoming a threat to them. If he backs off and does nothing, he risks looking as if he doesn't care or, worse yet, as if he is negligent. In the process, he may jeopardize his pastoral relationship with some. Eventually, however, most parents will be grateful for the help.

To my relief, Donald's mother called soon after Christmas to say that the psychiatrist they were seeing had convinced her that Donald was lying and that they were planning to continue weekly therapy sessions.

In January 1989, the state police notified me that, due to the psychiatrist's efforts, Donald had confessed to very minor offenses against three children. It was the break we had been praying for.

Due to the slow inner workings of the judicial system, it took until May for Donald to appear in court, where he pled guilty to a plea-bargained, single count of second-degree criminal sexual conduct. He was ordered to undergo therapy as a ward of the court and was placed in a residential treatment center for young male sex offenders. The grip of Donald's denial had been loosened, but it wouldn't be broken for another six months.

One family found it easier to leave the church than to come out of denial. The father, when notified by the court that Donald had confessed to molesting the man's child, came straight from work to my office. Not only did he want to ignore the whole thing; he wanted to keep it from his wife as well. She had been very ill, and he feared the news would cause her to have an emotional breakdown.

Even if he could somehow resolve the ethical issue of not telling her, I didn't see how he could keep her from finding out through some other source, and I told him so. I also voiced my concern about the harm this could do to his child. I promised not to interfere with whatever decision he made, but I tried to assure him that the problem could be resolved. We prayed together, and I gave him a hug and promised to be available if he needed me. Although he had served actively in the church up until that time, he never showed up again. Denial had taken its toll.

Denial on the part of the victims was the most difficult to understand, especially for parents who thought they had open relationships with their children. Over and over again parents would say, "We talk about everything. My kids wouldn't keep something like this from me." But the fact is, not one child voluntarily told what had happened until months had passed.

Bobby was a mischievous, tousle-haired five-year-old who had a constant twinkle in his dark eyes. He was a precocious, talkative child with an advanced vocabulary. His behavioral symptom was a marked change in personality. He became quiet and moody and expressed violent hostility toward Donald. Although his mother was careful never to initiate the conversation, Bobby talked constantly of ways to execute or jail Donald. While riding in a car past a lake, he said, "They ought to take Donald out in the middle in a boat and dump him overboard." One day they drove past the county jail and Bobby mused about what a good place that would be for Donald. He even suggested that a fence be built around the entire state with police guarding it to keep Donald out. Even so, he absolutely refused to admit being abused. The police couldn't get him to talk. Nor could two different counselors over an eight-month period. Finally, after a year and half, Bobby broke down and told about his ordeal, but not until after Donald had confessed to molesting him. Even then, he would tell the worst details only to a police officer. Therapists explained that he was too ashamed to fully confide in his parents. Fear mixed with shame had kept him in private torment for months.

One family had three children who were molested and threatened individually on separate occasions. They kept their secrets not only from their parents but also from one another for about twelve months. After Donald's confessions, they were amazed to learn that each had suffered in similar ways.

Denial and minimization by some in our congregation made it difficult to deal with hurting families. Having been taught that problems exist only if you talk about them, a minority of influential board members took the stance that the parents were the real problem. If parents would quit talking about the abuse, they believed, the children would soon forget it. After all, the victims were just little kids who didn't really understand what was happening.

Parents of these children knew this was untrue and felt angry and frustrated that they had to defend themselves against such accusations. They felt abandoned and abused by the very people who should have been providing support. (This to me is a perfect example of "spiritual abuse," which would have continued to victimize these parents had it not been stopped.)

Incredibly, denial even caused some in the congregation to side with the perpetrator. Two families left the church, saying I had been unfair to Donald and his family. These two couples later found out that Donald had molested their own children and grandchildren.

Others took the position that most of the reported abuse was a giant exaggeration. Some thought the number of victims had been inflated, and others thought the scope of the abuse had been sensationalized. I even heard one person insinuate that I had overdrawn the case to attract media attention and become something of a celebrity.

Most people who thought Donald was exaggerating believed he was doing so to gain some kind of status. However, the very opposite was true of Donald. He was extremely uncooperative in his treatment program; and because of his reluctance to confess fully, it took five months for him to reach the first treatment plateau, something which others in the program achieved in six weeks. He consistently minimized his crimes and told as little as possible to get by in therapy sessions. It took almost a year to get the full revelations from him, after which he was tried and convicted on further charges. He had absolutely nothing to gain by exaggeration, and in cases where we could corroborate the details of his confessions, we never found him to exaggerate anything. This view was just one more manifestation of denial.

Denial in its many forms is a brick wall, standing in the way of helping many hurting people. Although there were days we despaired of ever moving beyond this wall, we did find that it was not impregnable. By persistently chipping away, we were able to move on to the important business of healing.

Before that could happen, however, we were nearly shoved off course by another major upset—when the community at large learned of the events in our church.

FOUR

Newsplash

How to Deal With the Media

From September 1988, when I first learned about an abused child, until the fall of 1989, nothing about our case was particularly sensational. In May, Donald had been convicted of molesting only one child. But in October, during therapy, he began revealing the names of other victims. He made these confessions a few at a time over a three-month period. By the end of January 1990, we were immersed in the care of forty-seven known victims and their families. Donald had confessed to molesting seventeen additional children but didn't know their names.

While we were still reeling from the impact of Donald's revelations, the news media crashed in on us. The trial of the McMartin preschool case in California was just coming to an end, and the media attention it attracted set the stage for our news to create a big splash.

On Sunday, February 4, 1990, our story hit the

news. I left the house early to buy a morning paper. Although I had read a computer printout of the article and knew they had named the suspects, I hadn't realized they would put pictures of Donald and his brother Peter on the front page. On the way to church we heard the news report on the radio, and I knew the story had been released as scheduled to the Associated Press.

When I arrived at church, two reporters from our local *Times* were waiting for me. Adding to our woes, the church had a history of antagonism toward the paper and at one point had mounted a boycott against it, so I knew their presence would alarm the congregation. Reporters were not welcome in normal conditions, and I couldn't be absolutely sure that someone wouldn't try to throw them out bodily.

I calmed the ushers, canceled my Sunday school duties, and invited the two into my office. After answering all their questions, I asked if they would mind leaving before the preaching service. They suggested a compromise. One would leave and the other would stay as a silent observer. She agreed to not make her presence known until after the worship service. Since I had no way of barring anyone from the public service anyway, I agreed.

Before the invocation, I acknowledged the news headlines and announced that we still hoped to center our attention on worship. I said as little as possible, knowing the reporter was taking notes. The service went smoothly and we were singing a final hymn when an usher brought me a note saying that TV crews were set up in the parking lot and that reporters were waiting at the exits to interview people as they left.

Our church members had been drilled for years to fear the "humanists" and "liberals" in the media; so to avert the possibility of an ugly altercation in the parking lot, I announced, before giving the benediction, that TV crews were waiting outside.

I assured the people that they were free to talk to reporters if they wished, but that it was all right to politely decline comment if they had nothing to say.

"I've been talking to newspeople most of the weekend and none of them have bitten me yet," I joked.

Despite my attempts to allay their concerns, a couple families were so intimidated that they had their cars brought to a service entrance in the back of the church and fled to their homes.

Media Phobia

Talking about any problem had been absolutely forbidden at the church for years. This was carried to such an extreme that even prayer requests for people going into surgery had to be couched in nebulous terms. If people making the request named the kind of surgery, they risked being labeled a gossip or "unspiritual." Anyone who talked about a problem was considered to *be* the problem.

I didn't want the newspeople to misinterpret this fear as an attempted cover-up. We had nothing to hide, and I wanted to be sure we didn't inadvertently project an image that made it seem as if we did. Apparently our folks took their cue from me, and we had no unpleasant incidents with any of the newspeople throughout the day or the following weeks.

Before the first crew finished that morning, a second crew arrived, and I did interviews through the early afternoon. Other TV crews arrived in the evening, and one of the morning crews came back. Their editing equipment had chewed up their film and they needed a retake.

I went to bed exhausted that night, but I figured the worst was over. Little did I know. . . . The next day reporters from around the state started arriving by car, camper, and plane. One crew even came in by helicopter. I spent the majority of each day through Friday doing interviews, including one with CNN.

Some reporters asked how we had managed to "hide" this scandal for so long.

"I reported this to the state police as soon as I knew it," I replied with some irritation. "And we have cooperated fully with Child Protective Services, the juvenile court, and the county prosecutor. The only people we didn't call were reporters. Did you really expect us to do that?"

That seemed to quiet them down on the matter.

Given the high cost a sexual abuse scandal can exact from a ministry, it is not hard to understand the temptation some may feel to simply hide the truth. While it might be possible to avoid public scrutiny when the incident of sexual abuse is isolated or the offender is not some prominent person,

I am convinced that it would be nearly impossible to cover up a case of widespread abuse. And if a cover-up was attempted unsuccessfully, the resulting fallout would be far worse than if it had been dealt with openly from the beginning.

Even the appearance of a cover-up can be damaging. The pastoral staff of one large church found out about a far-reaching case of sexual abuse at about the same time the papers learned of it. They were still trying to figure out how to announce the problem to the church when the headlines came out in the papers one Sunday morning. This opened them to the charge of hiding the problem and endangering the children of the church. That was not true, but it added further complications to an already complex situation.

Treatment by the Press

In general the press treated us fairly. The inaccuracies that did get printed were the result of poor shorthand or a rush to meet a deadline rather than intentional misrepresentations. The reporters we met were decent people, and not one of them cast us in a bad light or reported the facts in a slanted way.

We did, however, disagree with some of the decisions made by our local paper. For instance, we thought the decision to publish the names and pictures of the perpetrators was unnecessary and unwise. Although not against the law to do so, it was a departure from a long-standing code of ethics among journalists. However, some believe that adolescents who commit gross crimes should not be treated with this deference. We disagreed, and so did others in the news industry. And they said so in print. A paper owned by the *Times'* parent company printed an article critical of the decision. And a few weeks later a UPI story in *The New York Times* criticized the decision to reveal the names of juvenile offenders.

After the initial story everyone wanted to do personal-interest, follow-up stories, which meant they wanted to talk to the parents of victims. I had made it clear in each interview that I would answer all of their questions but I would not divulge the identity of any of the victims. To get around this, one paper from the other side of the state began calling every telephone number in our town, hoping to find a victim family willing to talk. That meant all of the townspeople were being harassed on account of us, and I wanted to put a stop to that.

I asked one articulate young mother if she would do interviews with me present as long as her name and that of her child were kept confidential. She agreed, and the compromise worked. The newspeople agreed to stop trying to locate any of the other families if they could talk to one parent. The television crews used backlighting so the mother's face was in a shadow, and the newspaper reporters gathered in my office around a speakerphone and interviewed the mother at her home. That minimized the number of individual interviews she had to give.

Despite her nervousness, she did an excellent

job of telling her family's story and of expressing her faith in Christ.

We'd heard plenty of stories about the liberal bias of the media, so we were expecting the worst from some of the bigger news organizations. Ted Turner, the head of Cable News Network, had been particularly outspoken in his criticism of Christianity, so we agreed to an interview with CNN on the condition that they not edit out the part about personal faith in God. They kept their part of the bargain, and Turner's organization helped us give a gospel testimony around the world. Friends called from as far away as Jamaica, Florida, Hawaii, and the Philippines to say they had seen me on television.

Before the magnitude of the abuse became known to us, we thought, perhaps naively, that the case might not attract media attention. However, as Donald's confessions mounted, our hopes of quietly handling the situation diminished. Our questions concerning what to do *if* the media found out changed to what to do *when* they found out.

The County Sex Abuse Task Force met for a strategy session on how to deal with reporters when the time came. I was so anxious to break the tension that I suggested we give the story to our local paper. If it was inevitable, why wait? Besides, wasn't the case so old that it would no longer be newsworthy?

My naivete bemused the court people, who assured me that the magnitude of our case would almost certainly guarantee national news coverage. The judge recommended that we not volunteer any information. He hoped to keep the name of our church anonymous when the story broke. Our official board agreed with the judge, so I deferred to their counsel. But I continued to wake up every morning with a sense of foreboding, wondering if it would be the day reporters would knock on my door. It would be me, not the judge, in the hot seat then.

The *Times* picked up the scent of the story following a meeting between a victim's parents and representatives from social services agencies. We have yet to find out who leaked the information, however. Some believe it was a vindictive parent, but by that time dozens of people had access to the information, so it could just as easily have been a social worker or someone from the court system.

The publicity was devastating to Donald and his family. He had to be taken out of school for several weeks and was eventually enrolled in another school district under an alias. Peter, who had not yet been tried, fiercely claimed his innocence. He attended the only public high school in town, and the publicity not only divided the school against our church but tended to polarize the whole community.

The publicity put such pressure on Donald's mother that she sold their home, quit her job, and moved to another city, even though the move was emotionally and financially difficult for her and the children.

I soon grew weary of the incessant follow-up stories that everyone wanted to do. After a week I quit granting interviews because there was absolutely nothing new to say. Even so, for a solid year our local paper continued to print articles about this case, and it seemed that the name of our church appeared in print every month. Just when things would calm down a bit, another story would appear. At the end of the calendar year they did a "Year in Review" piece, and of course the name and picture of our church were at the top of the page.

The repeated publicity made it difficult for us to get back to normal. Even if the paper meant us no harm, and I have no reason to believe they did, it was difficult to see what good the ongoing stories did for anyone.

The reporter who stayed in our service the day of the original coverage called on the first anniversary to see if she could do a follow-up on how the congregation had healed during the year.

"We've hardly had time to do much healing," I said. "We've been involved for the entire year in court cases involving Donald, his brother, and their father."

When she called, it had been only two weeks since the last of them had been settled. That added up to two-and-a-half years that we had been embroiled in this case and a year that we had lived in the public eye. At one point we even seriously discussed changing the name of the church to avoid any more publicity.

Strategy for Media Relations

In a case of sexual abuse, it is unrealistic to think you can take a "no comment" stance with the media. Newspeople will find someone else to interview if an official spokesperson doesn't deal with them.

The best way to avoid distortions and inaccuracies is to formulate a strategy for media relations and to designate a ministry representative to talk to the press. With the integrity of so many Christian ministries being called into question today, honesty should be the guiding principle when dealing with the public.

There are, however, legitimate reasons for controlling the information that is released to the press; and your policy for what to say to the press, how to say it, and when should be formed with these in mind.

The number one concern of anyone in ministry is to protect the privacy of victims and their families. Some of the victims may have no problem talking with reporters, but most will want to maintain anonymity. Parents who agree to make statements to the press should be shielded from unnecessary stress. The number of interviews in which a parent has to repeat the story should be kept to a minimum. A press conference can accomplish this purpose, and it is a good idea to have a support person on hand to give moral support during a press interview.

Legal Ramifications

Another aspect of media strategy has to do with legal ramifications. No information should be given out that may jeopardize current or future legal proceedings. Also, exercise caution in saying things, particularly about the perpetrator or his family, that could be construed as libelous. Comment only on known facts and refrain from giving any hearsay information or personal opinions. Reporters will be very persistent in trying to dig up background material, but the safest course is to stick to the main facts of the case.

Seek legal advice if there is any question as to what is and what is not appropriate to comment on to the press.

Some media spokespersons may decide to issue a written statement. Others feel comfortable speaking from a written outline of the facts. Those who choose the latter should take time to review the sequence of events before giving interviews.

At the advice of a pastor who'd had a similar case in his church, I had kept a journal from the beginning. Whenever something of a potentially explosive nature comes up, especially something as volatile as child sexual abuse, a daily record of events is essential for keeping facts separated from emotions. I referred to my record frequently during the police investigation and when dealing with the press.

Media Spokesperson

The press will want to speak with someone in an official capacity. This person must be familiar with the case and be available for unscheduled interviews. The most likely candidate is the person on the pastoral staff who is working most closely with the case, which can mean the senior pastor and/or a counseling pastor. In addition to being knowledgeable, however, this person should also be articulate and have no known tendency to make impulsive comments or insensitive remarks in a pressure situation.

This person should consult with juvenile case-workers, court personnel, the juvenile court judge, and members of the prosecutor's staff to formulate a media strategy and decide what information to give out. These professionals are experienced in dealing with the press, and they too have legitimate concerns about the media handling of the case.

The County Sex Abuse Task Force kept me apprised of their own strategy sessions as well, and they shared my concern that we deal with this case in a concerted effort.

Spokespersons who choose to work as a team with the outside agencies involved in the case will be able to speak openly for their church without unwittingly complicating matters for those in the judicial system.

Conflicting Needs in Publicity

Tension with the media is not unique to the church. There is also tension between the press and the judicial system. In every stressful situation there are people who want privacy and others who want to know, or think they have the right to know, all the details of any case.

The judge in our case didn't want media coverage and ruled that cameras would be banned from the courtroom. Of course, the newspapers and television stations wanted the courtroom totally open to the press. The county prosecutor, an elected official, also wanted the trial open to cameramen and film crews.

The newspaper editor has to be concerned about profitability. And what makes a newspaper profitable? A sensational story certainly helps. And continuing to milk an important story for weeks and months evidently does too.

Newspeople have a job to do that requires them to intrude upon people's privacy. But without exception the reporters with whom we worked were well mannered and sympathetic. Several even apologized for having to disrupt our lives. Still, their need to perform their jobs was counter to our need to be left alone.

When Cranston brought me the advance copy of the story Saturday evening, he apologized for the grief he knew we would bear on Sunday. But neither of us could foresee how the news coverage would hinder the healing process for our people.

And along with the cataclysm of other needs, a leader will soon have to focus on the need for healing in the victims, their families, and in the whole church community.

FIVE

Healing

How to Identify and Treat Victims

An ounce of prevention may be worth a pound of cure, but I came on the scene too late for prevention to be an option. The abuse had already happened. So the job ahead was one of healing.

Prior to Donald's confessions all the victims denied they had been abused, so parents had great difficulty determining whether or not their children actually needed any help. How to question them to find out proved to be a problem in itself. Should parents persist in questioning children in spite of their denial? How does one continue to bring up the issue when the child refuses to talk about it? What if the child really wasn't abused? Could repeated questioning cause psychological harm to a child who is honestly telling the truth? If the child was obviously abused but refuses to admit it, how can parents phrase questions so that ideas are not placed in the child's mind or words put in his or her mouth?

Pastors and parents need to be especially sensitive to this last issue and make absolutely sure they in no way influence the statements of children and thus distort the truth. If any of the cases go to court, the outcome will hang largely on the testimony of the victims. An astute defense attorney can discredit a child's testimony if there is evidence that the child has been improperly questioned.

This became a critical factor in the outcome of one case. Billy Gifford, the chief witness, was a bright and energetic six-year-old who'd been molested at age four. He bravely withstood the various interviews and evaluations conducted by the prosecutor in preparation for the trial. Then the defense attorney demanded to interview him alone as part of the "discovery" process and adamantly refused to permit the mother or a representative from the victim/witness program to be in the room during the interview. This created a high level of anxiety for the parents, who feared the man would traumatize Billy with antagonistic questioning. However, the attorney spent only five minutes with Billy before deciding to advise his client to plead "no contest." The child's testimony had such a totally untampered ring of truth to it that the attorney realized it would have been devastating in court.

How to Proceed

In counseling parents who wonder if their children have been abused, it is best that you begin with a process of elimination. Is there any physical or behavioral evidence of abuse? Has a known or suspected perpetrator had access to their child? If the answer is yes to either question, there is reason for concern in spite of the child's denial. Even if there are no physical or behavioral indicators, the question of access is important. When there is a perpetrator and an opportunity, there is a high likelihood of abuse.

In cases where there is strong evidence of abuse, parents should begin by asking their children direct questions but in general terms. "Has anybody ever put his hand in your pants?" "Has anybody ever hurt your bottom?" "Has anybody made you do something you thought was naughty?" "Has anybody played a secret game with you and made you promise not to tell us?"

Many victims will continue their denial even when asked specific questions. In those cases, parents need to provide an accepting atmosphere and assure the children they can talk about anything they wish at any time. Parents must promise not to be angry with children if they recall something bad that happened to them. This attitude of "relaxed concern" enables parents to keep one ear open for further opportunities to talk, yet keeps them from forcing the issue.

Relaxed concern works in most cases, but it is a slow process that takes many months and yields only small bits of information at a time.

After Donald's full confessions, parents were able to confront their children with his admissions. They were still careful to not give the children all the details, however, lest they jeopardize later court proceedings. Instead, parents would say, "Donald has told the court workers that he did bad things to you. Now we want you to tell us just what he did."

This type of questioning serves two purposes. First, knowing that the perpetrator has divulged the secret relieves children of his threats against them. Second, it yields testimony that can be compared to the details of the confession.

Always take seriously whatever information a child gives. If it doesn't make sense at first, hold it in abeyance until more of the pieces fall into place. There were times when the stories the children told did not make immediate sense, and we were occasionally tempted to discount what they said. In every case, however, the facts given by the victims under these circumstances corroborated those of Donald's confessions.

One boy talked about being stabbed with a needle, but he never showed any bleeding or puncture wounds. We learned later that a pen had been used for anal penetration.

A little girl talked about a dinosaur hurting her. Since dinosaurs were a popular motif in children's clothing and toys at the time, we thought she was just confusing two separate issues. Later we learned that she had been penetrated with a small plastic dinosaur that had a long neck and tail.

One little boy who was interviewed by the police on several occasions gave a detailed description of what had happened to him, but each time he gave a different story. He seemed confused about the time and place of the abuse. We eventually found out that he was describing three separate occasions. Like many children, he had not yet developed a concept of passing time. So when asked to describe how he had been abused, he chose randomly from the events stored in his memory. Eventually the police were able to piece together information that at first seemed contradictory but which made perfect sense when viewed from a child's point of view.

As soon as parents are convinced that their child has been abused, they begin asking questions. Will we need professional help? If so, what type? Should we see a doctor? Should we find a counselor? Will counseling take weeks and months? Will it be expensive? Will our health insurance policy cover the costs?

Medical Examinations

All parents who suspect their child has been sexually abused should schedule a medical exam for the child and an initial evaluation by a counseling specialist if the child shows behavioral symptoms. The doctor will check for physical damage and sexually transmitted diseases, and the therapist will evaluate the need for further professional counseling.

Medical evidence of sexual abuse is not always present, and even when it is it may go unnoticed or be misinterpreted. Nevertheless, an examination by a physician is important for several reasons. Sexually transmitted diseases (STDs) are an increasing menace. Among the twenty or so different STDs, the most common are chlamydia, herpes, gonorrhea, genital warts, syphilis, hepatitis B, crabs, trichomoniasis, and HIV. More than 4 million people contract chlamydia each year. Thirty million Americans have genital herpes, and 500,000 new cases occur yearly. The statistics are equally alarming for several of the other illnesses in this group. Lab tests are used to diagnose them, and while most are treatable, some cannot be cured. Each has serious results if left untreated; therefore, all sexual abuse victims should be checked for STDs.

Penile, rectal, or vaginal injuries requiring medical attention may also be sustained. Even in cases where no physical injury is apparent, these children may harbor secret fears that they have been physically damaged. Older girls may wonder if they will be able to have babies when they grow up. Boys too may fear that their bodies have changed or that they have some kind of internal injury. This may be especially true if physical violence was linked to the sexual abuse. Seeing a doctor will help allay these fears, or it may reveal damage, if any, and aid in early treatment.

Due to the rise in litigation in child sexual abuse cases, there is an attendant rise in the need for supporting evidence. Because of the nature of the offenses, there is rarely a witness other than the victim. Medical evidence, then, is likely to be the only corroborating proof available to the prosecutor. Forensic medical specialists using advanced diagnostic equipment are now able to note even minute, residual scarring that would otherwise go undetected. Medical technicians trained in the use of this state-of-the-art equipment can provide expert testimony in court. Clinics specializing in this kind of medical evaluation are becoming available in various locations. We had two within a sixty-mile radius of us.

Therapy

Rather than recommend specific counselors, a pastor can act as a source of information for the various kinds of services available in the community. Even if a pastor is professionally trained and feels competent, there may be occasions when it is helpful to involve a good counselor from outside the church milieu. In many cases, children need only one trip to a professional. Other children, however, will struggle with fear, anger, lack of trust, shame, aggression, or rage. These will require more than a single visit with a therapist.

Ideally, the pastor will stay in close contact with those who choose extended counseling so he can monitor the progress of the victims and stay informed about the content of the sessions.

A therapist used by one of our families began using printed material that pictured a home situation where two lesbians were rearing a child. When the parents objected to the booklet, the therapist ridiculed them for their bigotry. Because I had kept in touch, I was able to discuss these kinds of issues with parents and help them evaluate the help they were receiving. Through trial and error we eventually targeted several counseling sources that were extremely helpful.

Getting professional help for hurting children was complicated by the strong opposition to the use of non-Christian counselors by some on the official church board. They also blocked my proposal to use benevolent funds to help families pay for medical and psychological evaluations not covered by insurance. In their thinking, intervention by outside sources should never be allowed.

The congregation had been conditioned for years to have an "us-versus-them" mentality. The technique used to unify the congregation was to mobilize against "the enemy," and the enemy was any governmental authority, whether local, state, or federal. The county health department had not been allowed to gather immunization records from our school office, the fire marshal had not been allowed to inspect the building, the boiler inspector had not been allowed to do safety checks on the heating system, and no accountant had been allowed to audit the books for fear that the "government" was going to make the church close its doors.

A few of our leaders had been steeped in this peculiar thinking for years, so to them it was unthinkable to invite a caseworker from the County Department of Social Services into our building. It was equally unthinkable that I would "permit" parents to choose to take their children to secular counselors. They were also ill at ease with my frequent contact with the juvenile court and the prosecutor's office. When state police investigators visited me in my office, I asked them to come in an unmarked car for fear the janitor would panic and lock them out of the building. It had been a long time since our church had been on the law-and-order side of an issue. Civil disobedience had become the underlying tenet of the philosophy of ministry.

While trying to be an agent of healing for victims of sexual abuse, I found my way blocked by perpetrators of spiritual abuse. Dozens had been abused sexually, but hundreds had been abused spiritually, and the distortions of this second kind of abuse complicated the healing process. It would have been simpler to separate these two issues and deal with them one at a time, but they were inextricably entwined.

Government and Social Service Agencies

Admittedly, the resistance in our church to using outside help was extreme. However, there is a general hesitation among Christians to turn to secular social service or government agencies for help.

A variety of reasons account for this reluctance. Some think a person unacquainted with the grace of God has no help to offer a Christian. However, this is a misconception. The basic problems that need to be addressed are the same for Christians and non-Christians alike.

Counseling children requires expertise in understanding their vocabulary and thought processes and in drawing out of them what they think and how they feel. Pastors accustomed to dealing with abstract theological concepts may be at a disadvantage in working with children. If an inexperienced pastor counsels the child or advises the parents to forego the child's counseling altogether rather than see a secular therapist, the results could be devastating to the victim. A better alternative would be to supplement the child's clinical care by a trained professional with biblical, pastoral counsel to the parents.

Another hesitancy may come from the misconception that Christians must maintain an image of perfection lest they present a poor witness to the world. According to this view, to turn to outsiders for help is tantamount to saying the Gospel doesn't work. However, unbelievers who might be drawn to this "Pollyanna" image are not being drawn to true Christianity. It is a better witness to honestly admit our struggles and show that the difference Christ makes is in how He enables us to handle difficulties common to everyone. Unchurched people who cannot relate to a church's image of perfection can certainly relate to the struggles of life. Furthermore, the Holy Spirit does not need or want us hiding the truth in a misguided attempt to protect the integrity of the Gospel.

Although skilled Christian counselors are always preferable, they are not available in all locations. In many ways, we would have had no place to turn for help if there had been no community based social agencies in place. I marveled at the selfless way many of the social workers gave of their time—both on and off the job—to help us.

When people need help there is no time for philosophical debate as to whether or not to use secular sources. People in ministry would do well to think through this issue prior to a moment of crisis and to acquaint themselves with all available resources. This can be done in a number of ways: by attending seminars offered for this purpose; by reading public relations literature; by talking directly with the agency directors. The local Department of Social Services or any agency that deals with children can put you in touch with the resources in your community.

The pastor's role in the healing process varies according to the need and his level of personal competence. I had training and experience as a pastoral counselor, so I felt comfortable dealing directly with parents on issues such as anger and forgiveness. Where I didn't have specific training or ability, such as in counseling small children, I acted as a facilitator to link people with other professionals. When asked questions for which I had no answers, I admitted I didn't know and did my best to find someone who did. This enabled our people to tap into a variety of quality resources to aid the healing process.

Professional Counseling

Initially, counseling may be used as a tool to determine the fact or the extent of abuse. Children sometimes feel more freedom in expressing these things to a sympathetic authority figure outside the immediate family or circle of friends.

Beyond this forensic use, the main goal of counseling is to get the child to express feelings and thoughts about the abuse. Issues such as fear, mistrust, anger, guilt, shame, disgust, rage, and depression can be brought into the open. The victim and family members can be taught how to deal with these issues as well as with the general dynamics of abuse as they come up in the larger context of home, school, and church. Parents will need insight into the child's behavior to know how to properly respond to it. They may also need help in resolving their own feelings of guilt and anxiety.

Parents and those close to the abused child will have strong emotional reactions to the description of deviant sex acts. A child who is sensitive to the emotional response of parents may keep feelings inside rather than cause this reaction in his or her parents. Counselors, on the other hand, have been trained to be supportive without projecting horror, revulsion, or other negative emotions to the child.

Counselors also have a variety of tools and activities—books, videos, games—with which to put the child at ease and provide a caring atmosphere where feelings can be expressed and problems worked out. They are also able to give specific training in the area of prevention.

Who Needs Counseling

Some children will be much more traumatized by the abuse than others. Experts generally agree that several variables determine the severity of the impact of sexual abuse on a child.

Reaction to the abuse by the parents and other

people important to the child. This may be the most significant variable in whether or not the abuse has lifelong destructive consequences. Children should be reassured that their parents believe them, are sorry the abuse happened, will protect them, and continue to love them. It should be stressed to children that they did the right thing in telling and that the abuse was not their fault. They should be allowed to talk about their feelings toward the offender, but parents should not become obsessed with getting revenge. This could have the reverse effect in that it may make children feel responsible for getting the offender into trouble.

The relationship of the victim to the offender. The general rule is that the closer the relationship the greater the trauma. However, the victim's perception of the relationship is what determines closeness. Someone who seems to the parents to be a casual acquaintance may be seen by the child as a very close friend, or vice versa.

Duration of the abuse. Those abused over a longer period of time are more likely to suffer greater harm.

Type of sex acts. Again, this must be seen from the child's viewpoint. Something that is repugnant to an adult may not seem nearly so offensive to the child, or vice versa.

Level of aggression. Aggressive abuse is the most harmful, especially when physical violence is used.

Child's age and developmental level at the time of the abuse. A young child may not fully realize what happened and thus suffer less trauma.

Child's personality. Some children seem to have more natural ability to cope with trauma than others.

The need for professional intervention will be much greater for some than others. Counseling is especially important for children who:

- have suffered repeated abuse over a long time
- have been abused by more than one offender
- have been victims of incest
- have been highly traumatized by the abuse due to violence or humiliation
- show pronounced behavioral symptoms such as nightmares, bed-wetting, extreme fears
- will likely be called to testify in court proceedings

Long-term Emotional Effects of Abuse

Even after the immediate symptoms of abuse are alleviated, parents will have to deal with problems that may continue to plague the victim for years into the future. Although child victims are not automatically consigned to a terrible fate for the rest of their lives, there are possible consequences that parents and children's workers should be aware of.

Peer problems. Victims lose a part of childhood—innocence—and it can never be regained. They may sense, therefore, that they no longer fit in with their peers. Their knowledge and experience have given them concerns that their peers will not face for years. This in turn could create other adjustment problems.

Low self-esteem. Victims may find it difficult to shake the notion that they are defective. They may feel damaged emotionally as well as physically. This could lead to behavioral problems such as drug and alcohol abuse, sexual promiscuity, or becoming a sexual abuser themselves.

Depression. This could have its root in anger toward parents for not protecting them or at God for allowing the abuse to occur. It can lead to thoughts of suicide or running away.

Sexual difficulties. Because they have been prematurely introduced to sexuality in a very negative way, victims may have trouble with sexuality later in life. Starting junior high school, going through puberty, beginning to date, and getting married may be times when they again wrestle with some of the abuse issues.

These are areas of potential problems for which parents should be on the lookout. However, the prognosis is good that abused children will grow up normally if they are surrounded by people who agree that they are not defective because of what happened to them. Being a victim means someone else is at fault. The warm, loving support of significant adults will go a long way in counteracting the possible negative repercussions of sexual abuse.

Support Groups for Parents of Child Sexual Abuse Victims

Children are not the only ones wounded by sexual abuse. Their parents have needs that also demand attention. Parents tend to go through stages of grief that begin with denial and then pass through anger, sadness, and on to forgiveness and resolution.

When several families are involved in a case of sexual abuse, a support group may be of benefit. Because the facts in such cases surface over a period of time, people will be at different stages of the grief process for a number of years. In a support group, people in the more advanced stages can help those in the earlier stages. The pastor, if qualified, or a professional counselor can provide leadership that will keep the group on a course toward healing.

Although a support group should not be considered a substitute for personal, biblical counseling, it can be a valuable supplement to it. Subjects such as the righteous use of anger and how to work toward forgiveness can be dealt with very effectively in personal counseling. What isn't so easy to impart in personal counseling is a sense of togetherness that a larger group can give. Parents can see that their problems aren't peculiar to themselves and that there is nothing strange about their struggles. They can share their practical difficulties or emotional ups and downs in a safe atmosphere free from the threat of misunderstanding. Those who are further along in the healing process can encourage others to "hang in there." Knowing that others care and understand because they have had the same personal experience can be a steadying influence for parents trying to regain their equilibrium. Without a formal group, people may not know whom to link up with.

A group of this type serves several useful purposes: it relieves the pastor or other staff members of an impossible counseling load; it reduces (but doesn't necessarily eliminate) the need for professional counseling; it alleviates the feeling of isolation so many families experience; it helps meet two primary needs of abused families—confidentiality and encouragement.

Healing is a process, and families and victims need time to work through all the physical, emotional, psychological, and spiritual issues of abuse.

The pastor can facilitate this process in several ways: sometimes as a source of information and advice; sometimes as a counselor; sometimes as a sympathetic listener and friend.

Outside forces will frustrate and slow the process, but with focused and caring leadership, a wounded church can be restored to health and vitality.

SIX

Roadblocks

Frustrations That Hinder Healing

For the first four decades of its existence, our church had been a tremendous force for good in our community. Hundreds of lives were touched by its strong outreach ministries. The major emphasis was upon evangelism and discipleship, and the church was widely known as a vibrant, growing congregation where God was obviously at work. Then, about ten years before I arrived, a subtle shift in the emphasis of the church took place. A militant stand on social issues and an ongoing battle with local, state, and federal government began to divert attention and energy away from the church's original purpose. The vision for reaching the community for Christ dimmed as the focus of the church turned inward. It became a "closed system," which is a characteristic of a spiritually abusive church.[1]

---

[1]David Johnson and Jeff VanVonderen, *The Subtle Power of Spiritual Abuse* (Minneapolis, Minn.: Bethany House Publishers, 1991), p. 79.

As church leaders became known for their aggressive antagonism, church members found themselves increasingly isolated and eventually alienated from their neighbors.

Personal relationships were highly valued in our small village, and this reputation was a serious obstacle to evangelism and church growth. It was obvious that recapturing our former influence for Christ and restoring our credibility in the community would require hard work. We became very deliberate about reestablishing relationships with people outside our walls, and our efforts were just starting to bear fruit when the newspeople crashed in upon us. We were quite sure our public relations efforts would suffer a major setback, and it was frustrating to think of losing any hard-won ground in this arena.

We didn't have to wait long to find out the public's reaction. Monday morning after the initial news reports, we began to be inundated with phone calls and letters from sympathizers. Individuals and churches spanning the theological spectrum sent words of encouragement and assurances of their prayers on our behalf.

When it became evident that the community itself was largely supportive, we felt relieved and gratified. People apparently saw us as the underdog for a change. The news coverage had somehow conveyed a positive impression and communicated the message that our church cared deeply for people.

The cumulative effect was that our stock went up appreciably in the community. We rejoiced that

God had brought at least this one good thing from evil.

Harm to the Ministry

Although our worst fears about the adverse effects of publicity were not realized, it was a good news, bad news situation. The good news was that people in the community saw the church as a victim of a terrible tragedy rather than as the cause of it. The bad news was that we continued to lose people because of the abuse and found it difficult to attract new people due to the publicity.

Some of the people who left were victim families seeking a different environment for their children. Other people left in protest, saying we had mishandled the situation. And another group was simply embarrassed to admit they belonged to our church. I could hardly blame them because I too felt embarrassment when people recognized me as "the pastor of that church that had the problem."

Many who remained committed to our church found that they had lost their enthusiasm for inviting visitors to our services.

We couldn't shake the feeling that we had been stigmatized.

Because it took nearly a year and a half to arrive at the whole truth, the problem remained on the skin of our church like a festering sore that stubbornly refused to heal. Prior to Donald's confessions we had the difficult task of counseling parents whose children were possibly at risk. After his confessions, we worked with the court to notify parents of what he had actually done.

People we were trying to reach wondered if it was safe to bring their children to our nurseries. (Actually, because of what we had been through, our nurseries were probably the safest in the state.) Some had been warned before moving into the community not to join our church.

Some churches are known for their Bible teaching, music program, or special ministries to youth, senior citizens, or minorities. We were thought of as the church where "you-know-what happened." Even though we were doing noteworthy things in all the other areas, people didn't take us seriously.

Any church involved in a case of sexual abuse that becomes public will suffer both numerically and financially. A larger church in a dynamic metropolitan area may be able to rebound more quickly than a smaller church in a static or rural setting, but the effects will linger for several years.

This is not to say that all other ministry activities should stop or that new ventures should not be attempted. But recovering from abuse takes considerable time and energy.

The Simpson Community Church was especially hard-hit by the news of what happened at our church. Even though their staff had been working with me on our case for many months, the congregation knew nothing about it until they heard about it on the news. For them, it was like a terrible flashback of their own traumatic experience with child sexual abuse. It had been over five years since more than fifty children had been abused by a teen in their church, and they were still healing from some of the devastating results.

"Helpers" Who Aren't Helpful

We appreciated most offers of help, even though we couldn't take advantage of all of them. But some offers were hard to comprehend, much less appreciate. The most bizarre came from the perpetrator in the Simpson Community Church case. He identified himself on the phone as the "alleged" Simpson offender and insisted that I meet with him right away. He said he wanted to help us with our case and seemed genuinely perplexed when I refused to meet him or talk further by phone.

After his conviction at age fifteen, he had spent four years in an out-of-state residential treatment program. Following treatment he had moved back into the community. When he came into contact with his victims and their families, he seemed to have no comprehension of the emotional distress he was inflicting on them. Had I not known about this young man and the trouble he was continuing to cause at Simpson, I might have mistaken him for a repentant, rehabilitated Christian who wanted to turn his mistake into an opportunity to help others.

Each church or ministry will move at its own pace in the healing process, and leaders must exercise discernment in opening themselves to outside help. We especially appreciated those who offered a specific kind of help but let us choose when to take them up on the offer. Some we called upon immediately, others we filed for later reference, and some we rejected out of hand.

Not everyone who claims to have something to offer really does. Evaluate every offer, but don't feel pressured to accept every one.

Dealing With People Outside the Church

After the first few days of that first week of news coverage, I began to worry less about the adverse effect of the publicity on our ministry. Then I received an antagonistic call that shot my anxiety level back up. An irate father who lived next door to Donald's family claimed he represented an ad hoc committee of neighbors. Reporters had been knocking on their doors trying to get details for their stories. These families had gotten together and decided to publicly accuse us of a cover-up because we had not warned them of danger to their own children.

I explained as apologetically as I could that I had gone to great lengths to warn everyone I could think of, but that I honestly had never thought of people who were not a part of our congregation. To our knowledge, Donald had never molested anybody who was not in some way connected to the church. I also suggested to the man that perhaps the police or the prosecutor should be the object of their ire. After all, we were not responsible for the official investigation.

"I can't keep you from making statements to the press," I said, "but before you do, please talk to the people at juvenile court and the prosecutor's office." I referred him to specific people in those agencies with whom we had worked from the beginning. I knew they would convince him that we had done our best to protect children and that any oversight was not intentional or malicious.

After about an hour my upset caller seemed mollified. He apologized for his belligerent attitude and promised to report to his group that we had not acted negligently.

We organized special meetings for our own people so they could hear expert information about dealing with child sexual abuse, but it was impossible to offer this kind of help to people outside our church. We had no way of identifying concerned outsiders until they contacted us, usually one at a time.

News reports had stated that Donald had seventeen victims who were yet unnamed. We had already dealt with our own members about this, but for several weeks we received frantic calls from outsiders who feared their children were among these unidentified victims. Most had attended our church at one time or another but were no longer associated with us. Some had sent their children to Sunday school on our bus or with a neighbor. Others had visited during vacations and lived hundreds of miles from us.

Although I could not make positive identifications for these callers, I was able to be of some help to each of them. My first step was to eliminate those children who couldn't possibly have been involved. Some, for instance, had been in our church so many years before that Donald would have been a baby. For those whose children might have been accessible to Donald, I described physical and behavioral symptoms for which we had been trained to look. I tentatively eliminated those who showed no signs of abuse but advised parents to keep their eyes open in case any symptoms should crop up later.

Finally, there were those who had definite warning signs, and I tried to be as candid as I could with them. I explained techniques that our parents had found helpful in questioning young victims and talked about the harmful effects of denial and minimization. Although I didn't have an ongoing relationship with these people, I was concerned that they get experienced support. I always tried to put them in touch with professionals and made myself personally available to them by phone if any further questions arose.

Working with outsiders further taxes pastors or counselors who already have more than enough to keep them busy helping their members. They may be tempted to brush these people off lightly or to give them false assurances to avoid any further hassles. However, in doing so they may be ignoring a child who needs help or failing a family who doesn't know where else to turn.

I tried to treat these faceless people on the other end of the phone line with the same care and honesty as I did members of our congregation. Their concern for their children was justified, and calling us for further information was the right thing to do.

Frustrations With the Legal System

Although we appreciated the dozens of individuals who worked with us in the legal system, we found the system itself to be very frustrating. At times the people in the Department of Social Services, the police, the prosecutor's office, and the court seemed unresponsive. This was due primarily to their being understaffed and overworked. Unfortunately, the prospect for positive change in this area is not good, given the ongoing problems with state and local economies.

The court itself is like a slow-moving behemoth. Its calendar is always crowded, so a hearing date will likely be months after an arraignment, and the trial date will be months after the hearing. Further trial delays can be caused by both the prosecution and the defense. The prosecution may ask for extensions to gather additional evidence. The defense can delay the proceedings almost indefinitely with motions seeking such things as discovery of evidence, depositions, and changes of venue.

Then there are the frustrating complexities of the judicial process. The American system of justice is much more process-oriented than the English and European systems, which are more event-oriented. The American system tends to be so concerned with "due process" that the simple facts of the "event" can be obscured. Our system is adversarial; it pits lawyers against each other in front of a jury. The stronger of the two adversaries may win regardless of the guilt or innocence of the accused.

103

Added to this is the extreme difficulty of successfully prosecuting a sexual abuse case. The very nature of the crime precludes there being any witnesses except the victim, so the trial boils down to the word of the accuser against the word of the accused. When the victim/witness is a child, the trial becomes even more complex.

To begin with, children under the age of five generally are not good witnesses in court. Young children are easily frightened by the courtroom scene and confused about such things as sequence of events or concepts of time.

Defense attorneys do not have to resort to intimidation tactics to destroy the credibility of a child. They may simply show that the child is capable of lies or fantasies, or they may charge that therapists or parents have brainwashed the child. These and other techniques for dealing with child witnesses are taught in legal seminars held around the country.

In May 1990, as a result of increased pressure from his probation officer, Donald admitted further crimes against three of our children whom he had previously confessed to molesting. These disclosures were so gross that his therapist left the room and vomited in the hall.

When given this latest information, the parents of these children became emotionally upset all over again.

The Complication of "Root Causes"

About this same time Donald began implicating other family members. He accused his brother of molesting a boy at church. Donald's statement substantiated charges against Peter for which he was facing trial in June.

That case involved one of our young families, the Giffords, who had filed a police report against Peter in October 1988, soon after Donald first became a suspect. There was solid evidence that their son Billy had been abused by both boys.

Then Donald accused his father of molesting him at home. Although Peter and their sister, Katrina, had made incriminating statements about their father off the record, this was the first official statement anyone had made about John.

After Donald's accusation against his father, the prosecutor began to build a case against John. We were told that he would be arrested in early June. The date came and went, and nothing happened. Then we were told he would be picked up in early July. Again, nothing happened. On July 31, 1990, he was finally arraigned on one count each of first- and second-degree criminal sexual conduct against Donald, who was the only one of the three children willing to testify against the father. The preliminary hearing was scheduled for August 7 and the trial was set for November 12, 1990.

The prosecutor expressed relief that perhaps he was finally getting to the culprit who was ultimately responsible for Donald's and Peter's problems. His staff thought they had an airtight case, but after two days of testimony the jury deliberated and brought back a verdict of acquittal.

Public reaction throughout the community was

one of disbelief, and a lot of people wanted to know what happened.

The prosecuting attorney conceded that he had taken the jury for granted and consequently had made some strategic blunders in not calling certain expert witnesses to the stand.

The defense attorney, on the other hand, was very well prepared. Through a variety of legitimate courtroom procedures, he was able to prevent the jury from hearing testimony on several occasions. After the trial, one of the jurors admitted that she found it hard to follow the sequence of the trial after being dismissed from the courtroom so many times while the judge ruled on testimony. As a result, jury members were not sure "beyond a reasonable doubt" about the man's guilt. That being the case, they acted properly in returning a verdict of not guilty.

The prosecutor had hoped that convicting John would pressure Peter to confess before his trial at the end of the month. But the acquittal seemed to erase all hope of that. Peter and his father had the same defense attorney, and Peter would surely feel bolstered by his father's win.

Jane and Ron felt like giving up. The risk of exposing Billy to a court battle with this particular defense attorney seemed too great. However, it was too late for them to change their minds; their son had already been subpoenaed as a witness for the state. And they had already suffered so much grief that they felt as if they had gone beyond the point of no return.

After filing a complaint against Peter, they had

an unnerving time trying to get the state police to investigate. It took a couple of weeks to get an officer just to question their child. Then, unbelievably, six months went by before he ever even questioned the suspect. It was another six months before Peter was charged, on December 20, 1989, with one count of criminal sexual conduct in the first degree.

I had repeatedly called juvenile court and the prosecutor to see if I could get somebody's attention about this case. The court supervisor finally said, "You have a right to be frustrated. We're all frustrated about this. All I can say is that the system is not working very well right now." Or, as an assistant prosecutor said, "In these cases the only thing that happens quickly is the crime itself."

Peter's pre-trial hearing was set for March 15, 1990, a year and a half after the first complaint was filed against him. Sufficient evidence was presented at the hearing to warrant a trial and the date was set for June 18-19, 1990. As the trial date approached, the anxiety level of the Giffords increased. Billy, now six years old, would have to be prepared for the courtroom scene. There would be meetings with the victim/witness advocate, the assistant prosecutor, the defense attorney, and the court bailiff. He would have to be familiarized with the courtroom and undergo various competency evaluations.

Then, a few days before the trial was scheduled to begin, it was postponed until August. This was a psychological letdown for the Giffords, and their anxiety concerning what might happen in court increased in direct proportion to the days and weeks of waiting. A few days prior to the new trial date, it was postponed again—this time until early November. By this time I had canceled vacation twice because I'd been subpoenaed to testify. For the Giffords, the entire summer had been burned up in nervous anxiety. Again came the psychological buildup for the trial, and incredibly, again it was postponed. We all felt as if we were living at the end of a yo-yo string.

Peter, unlike Donald, fit the stereotype of a sex offender. During the two years leading to his trial, he constantly harassed the people of our church. At first he would park in our lot and visit with friends after Sunday services. This was extremely hard on the Giffords because Billy was terrified of him. Peter refused polite entreaties to stay away when children were at church. Finally, the Giffords got a court restraining order to keep him off church property and away from their children. After that he would drive around and around our block during services or park directly across the street where he made obscene gestures to people as they left church. He made physical threats to my own teenaged children at public school activities and harassed several mothers of victims by following them around town or acting as if he would run them off the road with his car. Yet, in spite of all this belligerence, he steadfastly maintained his innocence. In effect, he abused our people in two ways, first when he molested one of the children, and second when he traumatized so many people with his pugnacious attitude. But it was the slow-moving court system that permitted him the prolonged period of time to harass everyone.

Fears for Children Who Must Testify in Court

The American judicial system was not conceived with the idea that children would accuse adults of a crime and need protection from those they had accused. The Sixth Amendment guarantees the right of the accused to be confronted by their accusers in court and to question them through a lawyer. This safeguard for the defendant poses a threat to the emotional well-being of a child.

Seen through the eyes of a child, a courtroom can be a very frightening place. There is a robed judge with a hammer in his hand. A policeman stands nearby with a gun. The molester is seated at a table in close proximity to the child. And all the adults in the room look as if they are angry.

Before children ever reach the courtroom, they are subjected to a forensic evaluation to ascertain their ability to testify. Such things as level of intelligence, credibility, mental status, and family background are noted, and the report may be used as evidence in court. If a child is ruled to be incapable of testifying, charges are dropped, even in cases where a crime has obviously occurred. When a child is deemed capable of testifying, a child advocate may be appointed by the court to assure that the child's best interests are protected.

Children who must testify need to be acclimated to the courtroom and court proceedings prior to the trial. They should be familiarized with cross-examination and helped to tell their story in a simple and direct manner. Role play may be used, but care should be given to avoid altering testimony in any way during this preparation.

To lessen the trauma on the child witness, some states are working with videotaped testimony, closed-circuit television, one-way mirrors in the courtroom, and third-party testimony by professionals. However, each of these has inherent legal problems that are rooted in the rights of the defendant guaranteed by the Sixth Amendment.

Some states are seeking to expand the "hearsay rules" relating to testimony. Generally, hearsay testimony is not allowed due to the possibility of misunderstanding or misinterpretation. The exceptions are when a person confesses a crime to another in what is termed "excited utterance." An excited utterance is the first spontaneous utterance ("I've been raped!") made by a victim, with no intervening time for thought, after a crime. This rule has little value for children who often say nothing immediately after being abused but will wait days, weeks, or even months before telling anybody. Under the expanded rules, the first person to hear the first allegation of abuse by the child can become an "extended outcry witness" and testify in court on the child's behalf.

Pastoral Frustration

The overriding frustration for me was not being able to get closure on the case. Time and again when it seemed the situation was coming under control and we were getting back on our feet, some new wave would wash in and knock us back down. The repercussions had no end. It was difficult to live with the constant uncertainty, unpredictability, and the feeling that church life was out of control. For two and a half years the only thing that we could be certain of was that we didn't know what would happen next.

A pastor needs to get rid of his own frustration or it may cripple his ability to minister. The first step in handling frustration is to understand where it comes from. Frustration often results from unmet expectations, and many times the expectations were unrealistic from the beginning. For instance, do not expect to fully resolve the problem in a matter of weeks or months. There is no quick fix or spiritual Band-Aid you can put on the gaping wounds of sexual abuse. Do not expect the ministry to come through unscathed. There will be a price to pay. Do not expect to be free from having to face some of the same hurts and pains repeatedly. Victims and their families will go through a lengthy process of healing. Do not expect to have an easy answer for every question. Much of what you face will be perplexing, and people with more experience than you have still don't have answers for some of it.

If you can manage your expectations and keep them realistic, frustration can be greatly minimized and you will be better prepared mentally for the long haul.

Don't become so preoccupied with the problem

that everything you say and do revolves around it. Not everybody is as focused on the problem as you are, nor should they be. A hundred other concerns will be represented in the congregation. There are births, weddings, and baptisms to celebrate. There are illnesses, job losses, and deaths to be mourned. All the regular ministries must be maintained, and they all require your attention.

Maintain balance by keeping the subject of abuse out of public worship services. Preserve these times for corporate worship and spiritual refreshment.

When a church receives a "body punch" as powerful as sexual abuse, the natural response may be to bring everything else to a halt, but that is not necessary. The life of the church must go on, and it will as the pastor helps the body absorb the blow.

SEVEN

Tensions

Walking the Tightrope When People Disagree

In a highly charged situation, tensions will arise. Meeting the needs of one person or group may make it look as if you are neglecting the needs of others. You will be pulled in opposite directions, and whichever course you choose will at times feel like the wrong one. At times like this, ministry becomes something of a balancing act. Even though there are no pat solutions, there are ways to handle conflicts to relieve some of the stress they produce.

Making Appropriate Decisions

Tensions will immediately surface if the perpetrator and the victim continue to live in the same community, share mutual friendships and/or family relationships, or attend the same church.

One night shortly after the police first confronted Donald, he and his sister, Katrina, showed up at a basketball game at our Christian high school. Little Ricky, who was in the stands with his parents, became extremely agitated at the sight of Donald. Bob and Darla took him to the other end of the bleachers. When that failed to calm him, they left in exasperation. A deacon, seeing that they were upset, asked what was the matter. When he learned what had happened, he found me in the crowd and pressed to have Donald and his sister thrown out of the building. Since Ricky and his parents had already left, I suggested that we not make a public scene at the game. I didn't want to embarrass the two youngsters in public.

The next day I talked to Cynthia. She was very understanding and agreed to keep him away from public meetings at our church. This solved one problem, but in a small town there is no way to keep the victims totally isolated from the offender. Donald and Peter had the right to walk on public sidewalks, shop at the corner grocery store, and play in the public park.

The victimized children were terrified of the boys, so parents were constantly on the alert for an unexpected confrontation around town.

Appropriate Separations

Although difficult to implement, it is essential to keep the perpetrator and victim separated, at least at first. There may come a time when both sides want to attempt reconciliation. But until everyone is fully prepared for this, separation is the best policy. It is best for the victim for obvious reasons, but it is ultimately best for the offender also.

For one thing, the physical safety of the perpetrator may be at stake, especially if people see him as a continuing threat.

In one case involving multiple victims, two angry fathers threatened to shoot the teenaged offender. Before the police arrested the youth, the fathers went looking for him with loaded guns. Fortunately, the police found him first. After years of therapy, but with no apparent rehabilitation, the young man moved back to town. Once more his victims felt traumatized by his presence. The court agreed that it would be best, both for his own safety and the well-being of his victims, if he would move to another city. But he steadfastly refused, and there was no legal way to force him to move.

It is also in the best interest of the perpetrator and his family to find pastoral support and spiritual counsel in another church setting. They need help, but a pastor cannot effectively counsel both the offender and the victims simultaneously. The best way to help the offender is to work through another church. By doing so the pastor can stay in touch and check on him from time to time while leaving the major part of his care to others.

It is difficult to ask a family to leave a church, and tensions can easily arise out of misunderstandings about it. This is especially true when

115

innocent family members are hurt in the process.

Asking Donald to leave and transferring his care to another church did not fully solve our problem. Katrina continued to attend church and youth meetings, and Ricky and some of the other children became just as distressed at seeing her as they did Donald. I refused for several weeks to ask Katrina to stay away, thinking the children would settle down after Donald had been gone for a while. It didn't work that way, however, and eventually it became obvious that Katrina would have to leave if our children were ever to regain their emotional stability. This was a bitter pill for Katrina, her mother, and their friends to swallow because it looked as if we were punishing Katrina for her brother's wrongdoing.

I too was uncomfortable with the decision, but the situation was too volatile to allow it to continue. Something had to be done to allow things to cool down. As pragmatic as it sounds, the question boiled down to whether we should risk hurting one teenaged girl or risk continued harm to dozens of children.

I talked to both Katrina and her mother about the reasons for our decision, and they said they understood. I was kind to Katrina whenever I saw her in public, and on one occasion she wrote me a note of appreciation for this.

"Armchair quarterbacks" who think you are mishandling things may create their own set of tensions. We eventually lost two families who thought I had been too harsh with Katrina.

Leaders forced to make unpopular decisions

should be careful not to make them alone. One person's judgment can be clouded, so confer with others who are known for their spiritual maturity and wisdom.

When reasoning with your detractors doesn't help, don't take their opposition personally. Every leader faces decisions now and then that make life seem very lonely.

After the emotional heat finally cooled, those who opposed our decisions came to see that we had done the best we could do, and I was gratified when they told me so.

Appropriate Attention

Be prepared, at least in the initial stages, to spend an inordinate amount of time paying attention to the victim's concerns. There were times when I devoted thirty or forty hours a week to them, but I could not continue that indefinitely.

If you do not have the time or skills to deal with all aspects of their care, admit your limitations and rely on others who have proficiencies where you are lacking. For instance, I do not counsel young children because I don't communicate well with them. But I still spend time befriending them, and when they need counseling I refer them to people trained to work with children. It is generally more important that you be available for support than that you have all the answers to everything.

Appropriate Discipline

One of the biggest tensions following child sexual abuse has to do with the discipline of young victims.

One Sunday-school teacher came to me in frustration. "Pastor, our three-year-olds are out of control. The whole department is in chaos. We've never had this much trouble with this age group. How much of this can we attribute to sex abuse?"

This situation persisted for three years after the abuse occurred. An unusually high level of aggression marked each of the victims. It wasn't unusual for them to hit an adult in the face. One even slugged a police officer in the nose. Unprovoked, they would knock a teacher's glasses off, stomp on someone's feet, or kick them in the shins. They were unpredictable and could fly into a rage without warning.

A typical class might have one or two children with such behavior problems, but our classes were filled with them. Teachers, at their wits' end to keep order in the classroom, felt their last recourse was to call the parents for help. But the parents themselves were struggling with the question of appropriate discipline. Many hesitated to use any form of corporal punishment because their children had been beaten and slapped in conjunction with the sexual abuse. Different ones tried various discipline techniques, but progress was usually very slow. It often looked to the teachers as if the parents were doing nothing, which left them feeling helpless to control the class.

The effects of sexual abuse on these children were clear, and I would not minimize that at all. But even small children are intuitive about playing upon their parent's sympathies, and some of our children showed definite signs of being able to manipulate their parents and take advantage of their uncertainties. Teachers picked up on this and thought they knew better than the parents how the children should be disciplined.

Tension came in trying to be supportive to both the parents and the teaching staff without looking as if I were taking sides with one against the other. We didn't want our teachers to give up in exasperation, and we didn't want to offend parents by insinuating that they were failing in the discipline of their children.

Some misunderstandings in this area can be avoided by taking time to look at the broader implications of the sexual abuse. Our concerns centered almost exclusively on helping families in their homes, and it was an oversight not to deal with the group dynamics at church.

To keep these conflicts to a minimum, churches should gather the parents and all children's workers together for professional instruction about the residual effects of sexual abuse. This kind of meeting will serve three purposes. First, it will give everyone a clear understanding of what they are dealing with. Having some guidelines about what is reasonable to expect from these children will help dispel some of the uncertainty everyone feels. Second, it will fortify people for the long haul. Everyone is going to need an extra measure of patience and endurance. Third, it will help unite parents and teachers and make them feel as if they are part of the same team in helping these little ones through a very difficult time.

Having a professional conduct these meetings, especially the first one, will give it an air of authority that both parents and teachers will respect. A disinterested, emotionally uninvolved third party can bridge the communication gap between church workers and parents. In subsequent meetings, a qualified pastor or staff member may be able to act as a facilitator and build on the foundation laid in the first meeting.

Techniques for effective discipline should be discussed in these meetings, but everyone should be warned that for a while progress might have to be measured in inches rather than yards. One thing is clear, parameters do have to be clearly defined for the children. They will have to be told repeatedly that it is okay to be angry or scared or whatever, but it is never permissible to hurt someone else. How to enforce these standards will require some creative thinking because each child will respond differently.

Some children will respond positively to behavior modification techniques that reward them for good behavior, but for others this won't work at all. Punishment for bad behavior may include "time outs," where the child sits on a chair separated from the main class for a few minutes. However, this will not work for all children either. It may only aggravate some and make them even more disruptive. As a last resort, the parents will have to be summoned to take the child out of class.

In a large church with multiple classes for each age group, it may be possible to separate the victims so that no teacher has them all. But small churches don't have that advantage.

Parents of severely traumatized children may find that the most therapeutic approach is to drop out of Sunday school for a few weeks or months. While this is not necessary for everyone, those who choose this route should not be made to feel guilty or unspiritual. These people need a lot of love, acceptance, and special consideration.

Appropriate Response to Insensitivity

Another tension comes from Christians who cannot grasp the enormity of what these victim families go through, and consequently come across as being very insensitive.

About six months after the media splash, a Christian businessman and I were chatting in his office. He asked how we were doing and if things had pretty much settled down.

"Everyone seems to be making progress," I said, "but some families still face some pretty big struggles."

He caught me off guard when he said, "What's the matter with those parents? Can't they forgive those boys?"

Forgiveness, I tried to explain to him, was not the problem. Most of the families had managed to do that long before. But forgiving the offenders did nothing to solve the daily problems they faced as a result of the abuse. Some of the children had serious medical problems that were a huge concern to their parents. Some were experiencing social maladjustments due to the emotional trauma. Some even had developmental impairments that were linked to the abuse. Added to all this were the concerns over medical bills and counseling fees and how much their insurance plans would cover.

A wise pastor will deflect some of the insensitive or even judgmental remarks that come from brothers and sisters in Christ. In public statements and private conversations, pastors can educate the circle of people around the victims. Without giving names or specific examples, pastors can, in general terms, let others know the kind of pressures these families face. They can also suggest that the best way to comfort those who are suffering is by being good listeners and by refraining from giving unsolicited advice. On the other hand, victim families may benefit from occasional reminders that many hurtful words are spoken out of ignorance and should not be taken to heart.

Appropriate Response to Victim Families

Another area of tension that I never voiced, but which I often thought about, had to do with whether it was advisable for victim families to remain in our church. Some counselors advised parents to take their kids to a new church where the surroundings wouldn't constantly remind them of the abuse. Others advised that it was better to stay and work it through with the children, something like climbing back on a horse after being thrown. While I worked at retaining everyone, there were days I felt like telling them all to get away for a fresh start.

Eventually several families left of their own accord, and they seem to be doing well as a result. Others stayed, and they too seem to be doing well, which seems to bear out the fact that what is good for one is not necessarily the right choice for the other. Pastors should give people the freedom to make their own choices without laying heavy guilt on them. Talk over the pros and cons and help each family make sure they are really seeking the best interest of their children. Studies show that more parents than children want to move away from familiar surroundings after abuse. For children, the trauma of adjusting to a new neighborhood, school, or church may outweigh the negative aspects of staying put.

But those who decide to leave should not be made to feel as if they are deserting ship. Assure them of your continued concern and prayers and let them go with your blessing.

Appropriate Personal Response

The tensions that a pastor faces in leading a church through a prolonged time of crisis will take a heavy toll. People often ask how I maintained my sanity. Jokingly I reply that I'm not sure I did.

Gordon MacDonald's book *Restoring Your*

Spiritual Passion has helped me in regard to my own inner spiritual fortitude. One thing I have learned is that a time of crisis is no time to neglect private worship. The temptation to cheat yourself in this area will be strong due to the crush of other people's needs. But nothing is more exhausting and debilitating than trying to minister to others out of an empty heart. You must depend on the Holy Spirit to supply the spiritual stamina needed to go the distance. Your own faith in the Lord's sovereign control of His church must be unwavering because others are going to have serious questions about this. You must believe that testing can be a time of spiritual growth. You may struggle personally with God's will and need to find renewed contentment in God's call to serve in His appointed place at His appointed time for His specific purpose. In other words, you may find yourself wishing you were somewhere else doing something more to your liking. Your personal goals for ministry will need to be put on a back burner for a while, and you may need to realign your vision with God's vision for your church. You will face all kinds of things that require wisdom from above. All these things necessitate careful maintenance of personal spiritual disciplines.

It is also important to be disciplined in regard to your physical health since it can have an impact on your spiritual stamina. You don't have to be a jock, and you don't have to spend a lot of money to get regular exercise. I maintain a rigorous daily bicycling program that gets me out in the fresh air year around. My wife and I enjoy cross-country skiing and Rollerblading. Any kind of aerobic exercise will do, and you don't have to spend an exorbitant amount of time at it. You may be surprised at what twenty minutes of brisk walking every day will do for you. The important thing is to find something that you can (and will) do on a regular basis.

Along with exercise, watch your diet and try to get sufficient sleep. The latter may pose the greatest challenge, especially if high stress causes you to experience sleep disorders.

It is possible, says Bill Hybels,[1] to be spiritually and physically fit and still bottom out emotionally. Stress depletes our emotional reserves. Just as a run-down car battery must be recharged, we need to replenish our emotional "charge" when it runs down. Recharging takes time, and taking time off for yourself is not a luxury in a high-stress situation; it is absolutely mandatory for maintaining your mental health. Take a few minutes to unwind each day, and try to take a day off each week. Some weeks you may have to put in seventy or eighty hours, but don't sustain that pace indefinitely. If you miss your day off for a week or two, make it up later in the month. Plan a few weeks of vacation each year and consider taking several months off as a mini-sabbatical if you have gone through a prolonged time of intense strain. Our church gave me a three-month leave of absence at the end of my

[1]Bill Hybels, "Reading Your Gauges" *Leadership* (Vol. XII, Number 2, Spring 1991).

third year just to let me recharge emotionally. If they hadn't had that insight, I am sure I would have collapsed in an emotional heap.

Diversity is a key concept in maintaining your emotional reserves. Develop a friendship outside your congregation and deliberately invest time in the relationship. Go on dates with your spouse. Spend time with your family. Read a good book just for pleasure. Participate in your favorite sport. Mine is sailing, and nothing is as soothing for me as being out on the race course. Keep in touch with your hobby. I enjoy woodworking, which I refer to as "sawdust therapy."

By focusing intermittently on other things, you will find renewed energy to come back and deal with whatever consuming problem awaits you.

Many pastors have an *only-I-can-do-this* attitude toward ministry. If you're one of them, now is the time to ditch it for good and learn to rely on others. Call on laypeople as well as paid staff members to equalize the responsibilities when you are experiencing overload. You can't, of course, give away your own work, but you may find that some things you are doing should rightfully be done by someone else. Take inventory of the things you do that someone else could do as well or better and give them all away. Concentrate on what you alone can or must do.

When tensions arise, don't throw up your hands in despair. What seems unresolvable at first sight can be worked out through prayerful thought and considerate action. Give God time and room to work on your behalf. But also realize that in our less-than-ideal world, there will be some situations that don't have a perfect solution. When you encounter one, give it your best effort, trust God to care for the details that are out of your control, and move on. That's all God expects of you, and that's all you should expect of yourself.

EIGHT

Ethical Dilemmas

Finding Answers to Tough Questions

When the extent of Donald's crimes had become known the previous November, the prosecutor began exploring a second trial for him. Donald was charged with two additional counts of criminal sexual conduct in the first degree. The idea was to get the first-degree charges on his permanent record, thereby establishing a safeguard for the public when he became an adult.

This set in motion a new legal proceeding, and the trial date was set for three months later in May. Once again the prospect of small children having to testify in court loomed up. The parents worried over this coming date for seven weeks, but then much to everyone's relief Donald appeared in court on March 28 and pled guilty to both counts. The children were thus spared from having to testify against him.

When something as terrible as child sexual abuse occurs, it's as if a moral bomb goes off. The

129

ripple effect raises questions in many areas. In addition to the medical, legal, theological, and practical questions that arise, there will be some very perplexing moral and ethical questions to be answered.

You may need to rethink some positions you have held uncritically for years. Or you may realize, as I did, that you have never thought through some of the questions. Unfortunately, the heat of battle does not lend itself to cool-headed consideration.

In regard to sexual abuse and the church, four of the most perplexing dilemmas are: (1) What about prosecution of the offender? (2) Should a juvenile offender be tried as an adult? (3) Does it "revictimize" the victim to involve him or her in the ordeal of legal prosecution? (4) What about spiritual restoration of the offender?

Prosecution of the Offender

Does prosecuting a sex offender violate the biblical prohibition against taking a brother to court? This question was posed to me early in our case by the father of one of the victims. He said, "I've been reading in Corinthians where it says believers shouldn't go to court against one another. Does this mean we should just swallow all this abuse and not press charges?"

He was referring, of course, to 1 Corinthians 6:1, which says, "Dare any of you, having a matter against another, go to law before the unrighteous, and not before the saints?" Verse 7 adds, "Why do you not rather accept wrong? Why do you not rather let yourselves be cheated?"

This strong language from the apostle Paul comes in the context of a rebuke to Christians who were pressing civil suits against other church members before secular magistrates. Paul said it was scandalous that they could not resolve their differences within the church without calling upon unregenerate judges (vv. 1–6).

This passage has led some religious groups to spurn all uses of the judicial system and instead try to resolve every matter involving church members in a closed ecclesiastical system. This approach fails to distinguish between criminal and civil lawsuits. First Corinthians clearly deals with civil matters between Christians in the same church where they have recourse to arbitration, but it does *not* deal with criminal behavior. And Romans 13:1–5 establishes the fact that civil government is instituted by God to punish criminal wrongdoing.

Reporting a crime committed by another Christian in no way violates the prohibition of taking a brother to court, since the initiative for the trial rests with the state.

Sexual abuse is a criminal violation of the law and, as such, should be reported to a law enforcement agency. At that point the criminal justice system takes over, and any ensuing legal proceedings are out of the hands of the citizen. The police investigate and turn their evidence over to the county prosecutor, who in turn files suit with the court. The court will then conduct a hearing to determine if sufficient evidence exists to warrant a trial. If there is, a trial date will be set, and the victim may be called as a witness for the state.

This is far different from initiating a civil lawsuit and pressing for retribution of damages by the offending party.

In addition to being criminally liable for crimes, the offender may also be held civilly liable for damages to the victim. It is the victim's legal right to seek compensation from the offender in a civil court. We advised our victims against taking this extra step, however, because we believed it went beyond the biblical guidelines. In some cases civil litigation is unnecessary, anyway, because the criminal court imposes payments of retribution by the offender to the victims.

Even though our state allows a maximum sentence of life imprisonment for first-degree sexual abuse by an adult, some Christians still find it difficult to view sexual abuse as criminal behavior.

This point was driven home to me when we were dealing with Jody, a teenaged girl who was abused by an older man in his home where she was baby-sitting. The abuse continued for some time before Jody confided in her parents. When they confronted the man, he didn't deny the allegations but pressured them not to report him to the police. Then the parents learned that the man had a history of molesting teenaged girls but had never been reported.

Jody's parents came to me angry and confused. I recommended that they report the crime to the county sheriff, which they did. The sheriff responded immediately and by the end of the day had a warrant for the man's arrest. He fled town but was soon apprehended and jailed. Within a matter of months he was tried, convicted, and sent to prison for seven years.

Although the system worked smoothly and justice was accomplished, the case had several devastating results. Jody required counseling for over a year, her father lost his job due to pressure from an influential relative of the offender, and the offender's wife divorced her husband.

An unexpected side effect was that one of our deacons, a close friend of the perpetrator, blamed me for the breakup of the man's family. He accused me of precipitating the man's troubles by recommending that the girl's parents file a police report.

Eventually the deacon and his family left our church in protest. I doubt that the man would hesitate to report a person for robbery or murder, but somewhere he had gotten the idea that to report sexual abuse was "just causing more trouble."

Although this deacon may have let his emotions get in the way of clear ethical thinking, his concerns for the offender were not without good cause. When a man is sent to prison all sorts of difficulties arise. He loses his job and standing in the community. He may be subjected to horrible treatment by other inmates who typically look with great disdain upon child molesters. His wife and children may find themselves in desperate financial need.

His wife may divorce him.

Anyone with any compassion at all would dread to see these things happen. Shouldn't a caring pastor try to shield a man from the full effects of the law if possible?

The answer is *no*.

If the man is under your pastoral care, you should offer prayer, spiritual counsel, and personal support to him and his family. You should stick with him through his punishment, but you should not interfere with the judicial process. The state has a God-ordained right to enforce its laws and protect its citizens. The offender, by breaking the law, put himself in jeopardy. The person who reported it is not to blame.

It is always difficult to watch a person suffer for poor choices, but it is especially difficult to watch innocent family members suffer because of a bad parent or spouse. The church should give careful attention to practical ways of supporting the family while a father is in prison. This could include helping out with the cost of rent or groceries, finding a job for the mother or teenaged children, loaning the family a car, or arranging for someone to care for small children while the mother works. Some men from the church could befriend the children and provide a male role model until their father returns.

What If the Offender Is a Juvenile?

The law recognizes that some adolescents commit offenses once thought to be "adult" crimes.

Consequently, prosecutors can elect to treat an older teen as an adult rather than a juvenile. The family of the victim may be allowed to give input into the decision, but it is a moral dilemma that is not ultimately in their hands.

While juvenile court is interested in rehabilitating an offender through the mental health system, adult court is interested almost exclusively in punishing the offender through the use of prison sentences. The catch to rehabilitation is that not all youthful offenders respond to treatment. When juvenile sentencing ends, usually between ages eighteen and twenty-one, the offender must be released, even if professional evaluations state that he continues to be a threat to the community. The judicial system is not set up to deal effectively with the most seriously disturbed child or adolescent offender.

The pastors of Simpson Community Church pushed for their teen offender to be tried as a juvenile, but they later wished he had been tried as an adult. His release at age nineteen came just as the church was getting back on its feet. In our case, the prosecutor elected to try Peter as a juvenile. Before the case went to trial, however, he tried to have it transferred to adult court. But by that time it was too late.

Two convicted sex offenders wrote me from a nearby prison, objecting to the possibility that Peter might be sent there. One described in graphic detail the treatment that child molesters could expect from other inmates. He also pointed out how unlikely it was that Peter would get any therapy in prison. The few corrections facilities that have rehabilitation programs are so understaffed that there is no guarantee that every prisoner will be given a slot in the program.

Some argue that an offender under the age of eighteen is too young to be permanently classified as a child molester. The thinking is that he has not had enough experience to have formed a fixed sexual preference for children.

Even if this is so, he does in fact molest children, and if not apprehended and treated he is likely to continue the abusive pattern into adulthood. For this reason, every effort should be made to rehabilitate the youthful offender, which requires that he be tried in juvenile court. The fact that treatment is not always effective should not prevent the attempt from being made.

Turning an offender over to authorities is not tantamount to washing your hands of him. To the contrary, the legal system may offer the best chance of rehabilitation. In the case of youthful offenders the criminal justice system is the only avenue for therapy, and in the case of adults it is a God-ordained method for maintaining law and order (see Romans 13:1–5).

As much as possible, try to stick closely with the offender through treatment or punishment and make an effort to see that someone picks up the spiritual care of the offender when you cannot. For instance, it was impossible for our church to minister to Peter due to his antagonism toward us. However, a Christian family in another church took him under their wings and provided support for him before, during, and following his trial.

Re-victimizing the Victim

The system, by nature, frequently fails young victims. Even after the police were convinced crimes had been committed, the prosecutor was reluctant to go to trial with such young witnesses. The rule of thumb is that children under age five do not stand up well under antagonistic cross-examination. An assistant prosecutor carefully culled the list to find any child who would be credible on the witness stand. When Billy was the only prospect to emerge, the big question was: What kind of damaging psychological effect would a court battle have on him? Should a child be exposed to further damage in court to bring a criminal to justice? Or should the parents risk leaving a perpetrator loose in the community to spare their child from further trauma?

Opinions on this vary, but some therapists believe the court scene can even have a therapeutic effect on young witnesses. They explain that it is important for children to see that they are not at fault, that the perpetrator is. It is also a relief to children to see that the abuser no longer has access to them. Seeing the assailant convicted tends to reassure the child about these facts. But what if the trial fails to produce a conviction? Could an acquittal have the reverse effect?

Probably. So parents and their counselors have a judgment to make.

I recommend that you be nondirective in your counsel to them. Talk about the alternatives and pray together for wisdom. Is the risk of losing the trial too great a gamble? Is the price for seeking justice potentially too high to ask a child to pay?

Ron and Jane Gifford decided to cooperate with the prosecutor and trust the Lord to protect Billy. But they continued to pray that something would happen so he wouldn't have to testify.

After all Peter's harassment and repeated delays in setting a trial date, the Giffords' prayers were answered on November 21, 1990. Contrary to everyone's expectations, Peter's lawyer urged his client to enter a plea rather than face an entire trial. Peter appeared in court and entered a plea of *nolo contendere*—no contest. Later, at his sentencing, he was ordered to undergo therapy at a residential treatment center. At last the specter of any of our children having to testify in court was eliminated entirely, and we spent the first holiday season in three years free from the threat of legal proceedings.

It may be less likely that parents will face this dilemma in the future. In January 1992, the Supreme Court unanimously ruled that the Constitution allows others to testify on behalf of a child abused by an adult. This sets the stage for states to conduct criminal trials of adults charged with child abuse without requiring the child to appear in court.

However, if a child is required to testify, there are some steps of preparation that parents can follow.

1. *Don't project your own anxiety onto the child.* Children have fears of their own, and seeing parents handle the situation calmly will help fortify them.

2. *Tailor family devotions or Scripture memory programs to reflect on God's promises of protection and care.* Be careful not to focus on your fears, but accent the positive concepts of God's provisions for our needs.

3. *Take advantage of all the preparations the court makes available for young witnesses.*

4. *Discuss the possibility that the trial may not go in your favor.* Don't make the mistake of promising the child that his or her testimony will guarantee a conviction.

If the trial ends in acquittal and the offender is released, do your best to assure children of their safety. Try to eliminate situations that are particularly frightening. For instance, if children fear being left at home with teen baby-sitters, try using grandparents or other trusted adults for a while. Assure them that everything possible is being done to see that nobody will be able to hurt them again.

Avoid all contact with the perpetrator. In a small community this may be difficult. The last resort is to move to a different location.

Restoration of the Offender

The third moral dilemma has to do with the church's responsibility to the offender. Where does church discipline come into play? Is the church always required to forgive? Does forgiveness mean automatic restoration to ministry?

Your answers may vary from mine, but the important thing is to think through these issues so you act consistently with your church's policies and/or your denomination's positions.

The whole focus of church discipline ought to be upon restoration of a believer who has fallen into sin. "Brethren, if a man is overtaken in any trespass, you who are spiritual restore such a one in a spirit of gentleness" (Galatians 6:1). Therefore, the first responsibility of the church is to confront the offender concerning the sin and call for repentance. Due to the grip of denial and minimization that are so common in offenders, genuine repentance may not be immediately forthcoming. Give ample time for the person to confess the sin and forsake it, but realize that it may not happen until after a conviction or therapy. Months may pass before there is true repentance, and sadly, in some cases it may never occur.

In speaking of a man guilty of incest, Paul said to the Corinthian church, "Shouldn't you . . . have put out of your fellowship the man who did this?" (1 Corinthians 5:2, NIV). An offender who, after being given sufficient opportunity, does not repent, should be removed from church membership as a disciplinary action. Hopefully, this drastic action will produce repentance that will lead to restoration.

Those involved in sexual sins over a long period generally have fallen into a very devious lifestyle. Be on the alert for a shallow repentance, which may be nothing more than sorrow for getting caught. Genuine repentance will be characterized by several things. First, there will be a full confession of what the sin involved. This does away with denial and minimization. Second, there will be an admission of full responsibility for the wrongdoing. This roots out rationalization and blameshifting. Third, there will be a sense of sorrow over the damage done to the victim and a willingness to ask for forgiveness.

In looking for these signs of repentance, check with the person's family members and friends. If they see signs of a genuine change of heart, you can have more confidence in it.

When an offender repents and asks forgiveness, it is the responsibility of the church to restore him to fellowship. Evidently the Corinthian church was slow to do this. Paul admonished them, "This punishment which was inflicted by the majority is sufficient for such a man, so that, on the contrary, you ought rather to forgive and comfort him, lest perhaps such a one be swallowed up with too much sorrow. Therefore I urge you to reaffirm your love to him" (2 Corinthians 2:6–8).

But some questions persist. Does forgiveness and restoration to fellowship mean that the offender ought also to be restored to a place of service in the church? And should such a person ever be restored to ministering to children?

Soon after moving to a new church a pastor I know found that he had inherited a problem involving these issues. A man in their church had been convicted of fondling a preteen girl and had served a short jail sentence for the offense. The trial and jail term devastated Jess, and he experienced a definite turnaround in his life. His family and friends were convinced of his repentance, and the church permitted him to continue leading a children's ministry. When my pastor friend came on the scene, the church had a high level of ambivalence about Jess's area of service. People who didn't know him well were uncomfortable having him work with children.

The pastor talked through the problem with Jess, and Jess agreed to move into another area of service. The new ministry, though not his first choice, was one that used his gifts without raising questions of propriety. Jess's willingness to submit his desires to the best interests of the church was a further indication of genuine repentance.

When trust has been broken, there needs to be an established period of time for that trust to be rebuilt. A genuinely repentant person will be willing to submit to this waiting period.

There is no good reason to use in any kind of children's ministry a person with a history of abusing children. This policy, though restrictive, protects him as well as the church and its children. It is to no one's benefit to put him back in a place of temptation, or in a place where someone could call the church's integrity into question. Any public knowledge of his past will erode confidence in your children's work. Also, if any further incident of abuse occurs, he will be the first suspect, even if he is innocent. Worse, if he should ever molest another child, the church might be faced with a negligence suit based on the failure to act responsibly on prior knowledge.

An offender who has repented and been restored to fellowship should, at some point, be restored to service after an appropriate waiting period. However, when deciding on the particular place of service, consider the gifts and talents of the person but give high priority to the safety of children, the confidence of parents, and the integrity of your church.

NINE

Prevention
Getting Beyond "It Can't Happen Here"

The phone message asked that I return a call to Ben Mason, chairman of the Christian Education Committee in a growing church nearby.

"We heard the news about what happened in your church, Reverend Anderson, and we got to wondering if something like that could happen here," he said. "We want to ensure the safety of our children, but we're not sure what all we should be doing. What tips would you give us?"

"You're already ahead of a lot of churches," I said. "Admitting that it could happen to you is one of the most important things you can do to protect your children."

Sexual abuse can happen in *any* church, and *all* organizations that work with children are vulnerable. What happened at our church can be used to stress to people the importance of vigilance in children's ministry. We were being careful, but we've learned ways of being even more cautious.

I talked to him about the importance of education, the need for careful organization, general guidelines for the nursery, some specific safety issues, and the selection process for volunteer staff.

As we chatted about selecting workers, I mentioned the importance of checking references on new people.

Pedophiles have been known to target a child or group of children and show incredible patience in establishing an opportunity to molest them. A scout leader or coach may work with a group of children for a year or more before abusing any of them. Men have been known to move into a neighborhood to have access to children living there. An offender might even marry a woman just to get access to her children from a previous marriage. By checking references you might be able to weed out a volunteer who has a history of sexual abuse.

Ben replied, "I know exactly what you mean. We've got trouble with a guy like that right now."

He went on to describe a single fellow in his mid-twenties who had moved into town from another state and started attending their services. He made friends easily and seemed to fit right in. He was eager to serve and seemed to especially enjoy working with children. Whenever there was a need he was right there to volunteer.

Some supervisory staff began to wonder if he wasn't just a little too helpful and too available. A little checking revealed that he was wanted on sexual abuse charges in two other states.

The church removed this fellow from children's work. As far as they know, he had not abused any

146

of their children. But they believed they'd had a close call and wondered if they could have been held liable if he had committed a crime at church.

These are very real concerns, and churches should know how to protect themselves from civil liability as well as how to protect their children from molesters.

Education

The first line of defense against child sexual abuse is education. Since so much of a healthy church's energy goes into ministering to families with children, church is a natural place to institute training programs regarding abuse. Deal with the subject annually in children's workers' staff meetings and include a training seminar for parents in your yearly calendar. Check with your local school district and Department of Social Services to see what training is offered in the schools and in the community. If no programs are in place, your church could lead the way in educating the entire community. Organize a seminar at your church and invite the public. Your local Council on Child Abuse and Neglect or Department of Social Services can supply literature and suggest speakers to get you started. A church near us did this with surprising success.

Raising the awareness level of the danger of child sexual abuse should be the first step in training. Even after people hear the horrible things that happened in our "all-American" setting, some still go away thinking "there aren't any child molesters where I live." This attitude keeps people from taking positive steps to protect their children. A healthy amount of suspicion is a good safety factor for any family or ministry. It is naive to think that just because your church (or school or neighborhood) is a generally safe place, it always will be. When you assume "it could never happen here," you give a perpetrator easier access to children. And denying access to children is the only way to keep molesters from committing their crimes.

Children need to know that it is never safe to follow a stranger into a car, house, or unfamiliar surroundings. They also should be told that some locations—such as movie theaters, public rest rooms, and secluded parks—may be more dangerous than others. There is, however, no totally safe place. So rather than warn children about "unsafe" places, it is better to warn them that abuse is possible in all sorts of places.

Parents should be taught to never take for granted the safety of their children. While children must be taught to protect themselves as much as possible, parents bear the responsibility for their safety. Never leave children unsupervised even in the relative safety of your home. Keep track of them in the neighborhood. Get acquainted with the families of their friends. Check out your baby-sitters thoroughly, and don't force your children to stay with a sitter they don't like.

Much of our abuse happened in places other than church. Children were molested on the playground, in classrooms after school, in backyards, parks, and wooded areas, in playhouses and tents, and sometimes in the child's own bedroom while the parents were in some other part of the house. The guile of perpetrators in gaining access to children is incredible. That is why the responsibility for safety should not rest primarily with children. They should be taught about safety issues, but those responsible for their care should be constantly vigilant.

Child sexual abuse in preschools and day-care centers is a continuing source of concern. The longest and most expensive criminal trial in North Carolina history recently ended in the conviction of Robert F. Kelly, Jr. He was found guilty of ninety-nine counts of sexual abuse against twelve children ages four to seven in his Little Rascals Day-Care Center. While the majority of preschool and day-care centers are safe places, the U.S. Department of Health and Human Services advises the following guidelines for parents to follow:[1]

- Check to make sure the program is reputable. State or local licensing agencies, child care information and referral services, and other child care community agencies may be helpful sources of information. Find out whether there have been any past complaints.
- Find out as much as you can about the teachers and care-givers. Talk with other parents who have used the program.
- Learn about the school or center's hiring policies

---

[1]Material quoted from *Child Sexual Abuse Prevention: Tips to Parents*, a copyright-free pamphlet published by the U.S. Department of Health and Human Services, Office of Human Development Services, Administration for National Center for Child Abuse and Neglect.

and practices. Ask how the organization recruits and selects staff. Find out whether they examine references, background checks, and previous employment history before hiring decisions are made.

- Ask whether and how parents are involved during the day. Learn whether the center or school welcomes and supports participation. Be sensitive to the attitude and degree of openness about parental participation.
- Ensure that you have the right to drop in and visit the program at any time.
- Make sure you are informed about every planned outing. Never give the organization blanket permission to take your child off the premises.
- Prohibit in writing the release of your child to anyone without your explicit authorization. Make sure that those in authority know who will pick up your child on any given day.

Perhaps the most important thing parents can do is to start early and establish open communication with their children. Get in the habit of talking with them daily. Make it a part of your routine to listen not only to what they say but how they say it. Be sensitive to how they are feeling. Create an atmosphere where the child feels comfortable sharing everyday concerns and problems. Ask children how their day went. Find out what they did when visiting a friend's house. Ask how they liked the baby-sitter. In other words, get in tune with your children and be on the alert for possible problems.

Along this line, familiarize yourself with the signs and symptoms of abuse discussed in chapter 2. Watch for abnormal behavior. Trust your child's word. Trust your own instincts if a person makes you uneasy or a situation seems unsafe. If you must err in judgment, err on the side of caution.

Early in our process of training parents, Linda became convinced that her daughter had been abused. The perplexing thing was that the perpetrators from our church had never had access to her. Yet Jenny was extremely antagonistic toward men and became distraught when she had to leave her mother on alternate weekends to visit her divorced father. These symptoms were at first excused as the normal reaction of a child to the breakup of her parents' marriage. However, Jenny also began to draw sexually explicit pictures and use language that showed sexual knowledge beyond what she could have picked up at home. Linda scheduled an examination by a female doctor who specialized in sexual abuse cases. Jenny refused to undress and wound up in hysterics under the exam table when the doctor approached her. She had obviously been victimized. Eventually the abuser was identified as a teenaged boy who baby-sat with her when she visited her father.

Linda handled this situation correctly. She noticed the abnormal behavior and didn't try to rationalize it away. Instead, she sought out knowledgeable people who could answer her questions. She was sensitive to Jenny and didn't scold her for drawing explicit pictures or using inappropriate language. Thus she avoided making her daughter feel that she was bad or "dirty" for what had happened to her. Linda had her checked by a physician who specialized in abuse cases (and showed further sensitivity by choosing a female doctor). Finally, and with some difficulty, she took measures to prevent the boy from having continued access to Jenny.

Parents also need to train their children how to react to dangerous situations, but again, they shouldn't rely too heavily on this training. The nature of abuse is that a more powerful person takes advantage of a less powerful person. Children are always at a disadvantage when it comes to protecting themselves from an adult who is not only more powerful but also more cunning.

There are, however, some simple steps parents can take with their children.

First, warn children (without scaring them) that sometimes adults or those in authority (such as a baby-sitter, uncle, or teacher) may try to touch them or hurt them or try to get them to do something that seems wrong. Sometimes these grown-ups call what they do a game or a secret. They may even threaten the child by saying that the parent will be hurt or killed if the child shares the secret. Emphasize that anyone who does this is doing something wrong. Give these warnings in the same context as other safety warnings, such as "don't play in the street" and "don't go near the water."

Second, teach the child about the privacy of his or her body. Talk to children about their private zones—the parts of the body covered by a bathing suit. They should be told to say no to anyone who tries to touch them there. If saying no doesn't work, tell them to yell and then to get away. It's okay to push, kick, or whatever is necessary to run from trouble.

This goes counter to what we normally tell children, such as "Always be nice" and "Never be disrespectful to an adult." Sometimes parents even force children to do things that make them feel uncomfortable, like kissing Aunt Gladys when she comes once a year to visit. Be careful about conditioning children to always be submissive to adults. They need to be empowered to refuse what seems unpleasant or uncomfortable.

Finally, instruct children to tell an adult. Tell them they are not to keep secrets from you, and if anyone does something bad to them that you will not be angry with them. Assure them that if anybody tries to harm them that they should tell you so you can protect them. If you are not available, they should tell some other adult right away.

In summary, tell them to say no, to get away, and to tell an adult as soon as possible.

Another word of caution is in order here. Be as direct as possible when talking about abuse to children. Euphemisms and unexplained terminology may go over their heads. One second-grade girl was trying to sympathize with a friend who had been abused. Her mother asked if she knew what it meant to be abused, and she admitted that she didn't. When her mother explained fondling and digital penetration, the girl exclaimed, "Oh no! That boy did that to me, too." Until then "sexual abuse" was just a vague concept. She needed to

153

have it explained in concrete terms.

Even some children's educational literature fails at this point. One booklet describes dangerous situations children might encounter by using cartoon-like animal characters. Children may miss the point entirely and merely conclude that mice and other critters have a lot to be careful about.

Incest

Church leaders and children's workers should also be aware that many children are at greatest risk right in their own homes. A *Los Angeles Times* survey of August 1985 reported that 10 percent of male victims and 25 percent of female victims had been abused by a family member. Incest can occur between a child and any member of his or her immediate or extended family. The most common type involves father and daughter or a stepfather and stepdaughter.

Incest is an indicator of other serious problems in a family. Professionals agree that although some incestuous families are out of control and experiencing multiple problems, many are able to maintain the appearance of stability and respectability. Even so, they tend to be isolated socially, having few contacts or close friends outside the home.

The mother may be passive and weak, although this is not always the case. The father may be a successful and respected member of the community and may even be highly regarded in his church. Some are even clergymen or ministry leaders. He tends to be very domineering and authoritarian in the home, and he often holds a very rigid moral code. This may stem from his religious background, conservative politics, or previous military service. In effect, he holds a double standard and may even stress to his daughters the importance of abstaining from sex with boys their own age, while he himself is abusing them.

Incest is sometimes viewed as a family matter in which outsiders (including the police) are hesitant to become involved. However, incest is criminal behavior that probably will not stop without some form of outside intervention. Furthermore, the perpetrator will very likely abuse more than one child in the same home. Since the spouse often acts as an enabler and because the victims are too fearful to report the crime, help must come from outside the home.

Elevate the Nursery Program

In some churches the nursery is treated as an afterthought, or worse, as a necessary evil. It is housed in a dingy corner of the basement next to the boiler room and staffed by any warm body who can be coaxed into taking the job. Most pastors pay very little attention to the nursery except when someone insists on keeping a cranky child in the preaching service.

This kind of attitude breeds contempt for child care and makes staffing, which is a challenge even in the best churches, even more difficult.

Nobody wants to be involved in work that is perceived to be a headache or meaningless. By

155

placing high value upon these ministries, however, church leaders can attract competent and motivated people to serve the Lord in these positions.

When was the last time you personally thanked your nursery staff? Do you ever praise them in public? Their work is vital to the health of your church. A word of commendation now and then will convey the importance you place on this work and help build a positive attitude about child care throughout your congregation.

The nursery ought to be bright, airy, and spotlessly clean. All the necessary supplies should be kept well stocked, and individual storage spaces should be available for each child's personal things. Toys, furniture, and equipment should be kept in good repair. Windows to the hall or dutch doors should be installed, and parents should be encouraged to look in any time. Look at your nursery facility through the eyes of a first-time visitor. Does it give the impression that children are a top priority?

The nursery staff should be trained and proficient. A well-organized program will have less danger of abuse than one that is run in a slipshod way. For instance, the schedule should be posted a month in advance, and workers should be called a day in advance to remind them it's their turn to serve. This avoids last-minute panic over absentees and the pressure to let someone fill in who is less than qualified. Require workers to be on the job several minutes before people start arriving. Parents serving in other areas cannot wait until the last minute for the nursery to open.

Abuse occurred in our church for this very reason. One mother in a rush to accompany the choir asked Donald, who was standing in the hall, to watch her child until the nursery workers arrived. He took advantage of the situation and molested the child in the bathroom. If the staff had been early, as they were supposed to be, there would have been no opportunity for this to happen.

Donald sometimes gained access to children by offering to watch them during times when no nursery was scheduled. We now provide a supervised nursery for as many church functions as possible. When no nursery is scheduled, we urge parents to make special arrangements for the care of their own children.

The whole nursery operation should be run with professionalism and excellence. Without a well-run children's program, it is difficult to attract and keep young families. But, most important, these little ones deserve the best care possible in God's house.

Abuse-Proofing the Building

The church building itself should be made as abuse-proof as possible. In our church we did some major remodeling to make the building less confusing. A neighboring church designed their new building with many safeguards learned from our unfortunate experiences.

Classroom doors should have windows so activity can be monitored from the hall. Nursery doors should be split so the top can be opened while the bottom is closed. This allows access to the room while keeping traffic out and children in. Infant changing tables in the nurseries should be placed in view of other workers in the room. Out-of-the-way closets and storage areas should be locked. Modular classrooms separated from the main building should be locked when not being used for supervised activities. Playground equipment should be constructed so that children using it are never totally out of sight. Traffic flow between main areas of the building and rest rooms should be as direct and unconfusing as possible.

Donald molested children in many parts of our building. He confessed to watching for a child to leave a worship service to visit the rest room. He would follow, lurk outside the rest room door, and lure the child into taking a shortcut back to the sanctuary. The shortcut disoriented the victim and led to some remote part of the building.

We now urge parents to take their children to the rest room before services begin and, if necessary during the service, to accompany the child to the rest room and back. We also have ushers circulating throughout the building to watch for suspicious activity. Children's workers are never permitted to accompany children to the rest room alone.

Protective Policies

There are several policies that should be in place for the protection of your children.

1. *Nobody works alone in the nursery.* It may

seem foolish to require two people to look after only one baby, but for everyone's protection there must be accountability. Other church activities such as camp-outs, weekend retreats, and overnight activities should be especially well supervised. There should always be a sufficient number of adults so that not only are the children watched, but the adults can be accountable to one another as well.

2. *Do not let teams of workers from the same family (husband/wife, father/daughter, etc.) work together without another person in the room.* We use teenagers only in conjunction with an adult, and we quit using boys under age eighteen altogether. Some professionals object to this last point, saying it is an overreaction. We recognize there are many fine, responsible boys who do very well with children. However, we implemented this decision to help us bring a unique and difficult situation under control. There may come a day when we will once again allow teen boys to work along with adults in the nurseries.

3. *When a parent has to be called out of a service to attend to a child, an usher, not a nursery worker, should do it.* This way, one worker is not left alone while the other goes to get the parent.

4. *Allow only assigned workers or their approved substitutes in the nurseries.* The only exceptions are for nursing mothers (who should have a special area set aside for this purpose) and a parent called in to calm an upset child. Workers should receive the child at the door of the nursery and deliver the child to the door for pickup. This avoids congestion

and confusion in the room and permits the workers to exercise greater control over all safety factors.

5. *Allow only the parents to retrieve a child from the nursery.* Parents must be trained not to ask for exceptions to this policy even though it may be more convenient for them to have an older brother or sister pick up the baby. In larger churches, the use of a numbered ticket system will assure that the right child goes with the proper parent. In a neighboring church a stranger recently walked in off the street and attempted to pick up a child from the nursery. A ticket system avoids this possibility.

6. *Do not permit any child to leave the room with anyone at any time other than the parent.* This means it is necessary for the nursery to have direct access to a rest room so that all the child's needs can be cared for without ever leaving the room. If there is no rest room in the nursery, the child should never be escorted out of the room by a lone worker. Perhaps an usher could be called in to assist as a rest room monitor. With older age groups the entire group can be escorted to the rest room at the beginning of the hour. We do this with our kindergarten church. It seemed awkward at first, but now that everyone is accustomed to the idea, it works quite well.

Policies, no matter how thorough and good, will work only if they are enforced. We had good policies in place when the abuse occurred, but some people didn't fully understand the reason for the rules and bent them a little when they got under pressure. Workers must be reminded from time to time why the rules exist.

Screen Volunteers

In children's work, perhaps more than in any other area of service, it is necessary to screen volunteers. Many churches are lax in this area, and some do not even require church membership. The church mentioned earlier in this chapter nearly got into trouble because they allowed a person to serve before knowing enough about him.

Develop a questionnaire similar to a job application. Some I have seen are quite elaborate, but they don't have to be. A simple one can get all the vital information. It should ask for name, address, previous church membership, positions previously served in, and the name of the immediate supervisor. Check these references to find out if there was any problem in the previous ministry. Ask the person to reveal any prior convictions and request permission to check his or her police record. Also ask for a signature and a driver's license number and social security number. These numbers enable you to check for prior convictions. Some insurance companies suggest that paid staff in church ministries also be fingerprinted as part of the application process.

These precautions may seem extreme; they did to me, too, at first. But I know of instances where the questionnaire has helped uncover someone with a history of sexual abuse. What about those who refuse to sign such a form? We have had some who wouldn't, and we use no coercion to get them to do so. But we don't use them in children's ministries. Instead, we suggest some other ministry where safety issues are not as important.

The questionnaire should be followed up with a personal interview, and you should reserve the right to reject from children's work anyone about whom you have doubts. There are many other less critical areas where people may serve. Those who do check out should be given a supervised trial period, at the end of which you or they can opt out of the position with no questions asked.

We had one fellow who was the picture of con-geniality—until he had to deal with fussy children. Then he turned into a bear, and his temper dis-qualified him from working with children. Others may be chronically late, more interested in gab-bing than attending to the children's needs, or un-willing to abide by nursery standards. Those who persist in unprofessional conduct will compromise your standards of excellence and undermine the effectiveness of your program. Just because people are volunteering their time does not mean that you cannot set high standards for their job perform-ance.

Civil Liability

Child sexual abuse is a crime for which the of-fender is tried in criminal court. The damage against a victim (called a tort) can also be cause for a suit in civil court. In this regard, the offender is not the only one who may face legal proceedings. More and more churches and their organizations are being sued for alleged negligence in three spe-cific areas: (1) inappropriate hiring of staff; (2) improper supervision of children; (3) failure to act on previous knowledge of wrongdoing.

The law as it relates to negligence is more clearly defined when applied to salaried staff than to volunteers. However, the most prudent course for the church is to treat all personnel, paid or volunteer, with the same safety conscious standards.

In one Christian day school a male teacher abused several boys over a prolonged period. When caught and convicted, he was found to have been fired from three other schools for sexual abuse. The church, which was found negligent, could have avoided a large judgment if they had done reference checks.

At a church-operated camp a counselor abused a girl. Her parents charged that the church had disregarded a previous offense and had failed to act upon hearing of the offense against their daughter. This church, too, could have avoided a large judgment by checking the counselor's credentials and by initiating a proper investigation as soon as they heard of the allegation against him.

To avoid being held liable for damages due to negligence, a church must show that they have acted prudently to ensure the safety of their children. This includes:

- Screening out known offenders. This necessitates the use of the employment application and checking all references. A check should also be made for arrest and conviction records. This can be done with the clerk of courts in the counties where the applicant lived and worked.

163

- Develop a list of protective policies that spells out the guidelines for adult/child relationships and communicate them to the staff, parents, and children.
- Conduct an immediate inquiry into all alleged incidents of sexual abuse.
- Report all incidents of abuse to the proper agency.
- Notify your liability insurance company at the time you report the abuse to the authorities. This allows the company to be prepared should civil litigation arise and will not be construed as an admission of negligence on your part.

Check to see if your policy covers liability for sexual abuse, because not all do. You may have to pay extra for a specific rider to be attached to your policy. If you are not sure about your policy, check now, because it will be too late after an incident of abuse occurs. Discuss with your agent the amount of coverage you should carry. One legal expert advises that three million dollars worth of coverage be considered a minimum. There are others who argue that carrying a large amount of liability coverage invites a lawsuit. My own opinion is that given the prevailing willingness to sue in our country, a church would be foolish not to have adequate coverage. A suit is typically aimed at the one with the deepest pockets, and even a small church will usually have greater assets than the offender. Why jeopardize those assets when liability coverage can be obtained rather inexpensively?

Although sparing the church financial jeopardy

is important, the issue that should remain foremost about prevention is the safety of children. If just one child could be spared the agony of abuse, no effort of prevention would seem too costly or extreme.

Epilogue

One of our departmental superintendents stopped me in the hall just before church one morning and asked, "Pastor, can you drop in on our beginner Sunday school class two weeks from today? We want to make sure the children know who you are."

"I'd be glad to," I replied. As I marked the date on my calendar, I noted an interesting coincidence. The last time she had invited me to do this was exactly two years ago, and I had to cancel at the last minute because it was the day the newspeople showed up. I spent the whole Sunday school hour giving interviews.

This time when the day arrived, I got to the room early and stood outside the door for a moment. I thought back on all the turmoil the teachers had endured. At one time, most of the children in the department were abuse victims. My musing was interrupted when one of the children recognized me and shouted, "Teacher, Pastor is here!"

A beautiful little girl ran over and reached up to hold my hand. With sparkling blue eyes that were filled with trust she said, "My name is Janelle. I'm four."

With that, all the children rushed over and crowded around me. A dozen chattering, happy, trusting little people wanted to show me their coloring pages and craft projects. Later, we sat in a circle and they sang a special song for me and recited their memory verse. As I looked into those innocent little faces, I thought of all we had gone through to protect them. And I realized that no price was too high to pay for happy, well-adjusted, and safe children.

A few weeks later, our kindergarten church children had a special part in our main worship service. They sang two songs and recited all the books of the Bible from memory. I was on the platform behind the children, so I could see the faces of people in the congregation. It was so good to see parents worshiping in peace, knowing that their children's innocence wouldn't be robbed.

Of course, these children are a new generation. The abuse victims are older now. It is also gratifying to see how well they and their parents are doing. In fact, some who suffered the most emotional upset are doing so well that it is hard to recognize them as the same people.

One family that moved out of state to get away from the scene of the crimes is now working with their state's Child Abuse Prevention League as counselors and seminar speakers.

Ricky's father, Bob, is occasionally invited to speak on how his family survived. At one time he was tempted to give up his faith over the abuse. He thought he would never see anything positive about their experience. But now he testifies to the power of God's sustaining grace in their lives. Ricky started kindergarten this year and gives every indication of being a happy, normal little boy.

Jane Gifford recently asked if she could take ten minutes during an evening service to tell what God had done for her family. Two of her children were abused, and Billy had also endured the trauma of lengthy legal proceedings. She told about several specific answers to prayer and the providential timing of God's provisions. She underscored the value of Scripture memorization during their family's ordeal and marveled that God had enabled them to heal in such unimaginable ways.

In contrast to his hostility and anger following the abuse, Billy, now eight, has become a well-mannered, self-confident young man.

As I scan scenes like these in my mind, I have to say it has been wonderful to be a part of these people's lives. I am grateful to have been associated with them long enough to see the healing process take place. The experience has given me a whole new perspective on pastoral ministry. I had always associated the shepherd's job of protecting his flock almost exclusively with doctrinal matters. I concentrated on preaching pure doctrine and protecting people from wolves bearing deviant doctrine. Now when I think of being a shepherd, I think of the little lambs in our flock who need protection from real physical danger.

Donald, now sixteen, and Peter, nineteen, continue in a residential therapy program out of state. From what I am told, they are making steady progress but still show little remorse for the intense pain they caused so many. We continue to pray for the full recovery of these young people who themselves have suffered in so many ways.

Our church is well on its way to recovery from all the problems that plagued it for so long. Our evangelistic efforts are beginning to bear fruit once again, and there is a renewed sense of spiritual vitality in our midst. We look with optimistic expectation to the future.

Although this experience has changed our lives forever, I am confident that we have learned lessons that will prevent widespread abuse from ever occurring here again. Our church joins me in the hope that by sharing our story, we will have a part in preventing child sexual abuse all across our nation.

Resource List

The following resources are listed as the kinds of places to find further help but are not necessarily endorsed by the author.

SECULAR RESOURCES

BOOKS

By Silence Betrayed: Sexual Abuse of Children in America, by John Crewdson. Little, Brown, and Company, Boston: 1988.

> This is an interesting book written in the style of an investigative report.

The Silent Children: A Parent's Guide to the Prevention of Child Sexual Abuse, by Linda Tschirhart Sanford. Anchor Press/ Doubleday, Garden City, N.Y.: 1980.

> Although this book was written several years ago, it continues to be popular.

HOTLINES

Childhelp USA
I.O.F. Foresters National Child Abuse Hotline
1–800–4 A Child

> Located in Hollywood, California, this nonprofit organization provides literature, crisis phone

counseling, help in reporting abuse, and local referrals for counseling nationwide.

The National AIDS Hotline
1–800–342-AIDS
1–800–344-SIDA (Spanish)
1–800-AIDS-TTY (Hearing-impaired, for TTY/TTD service)

The National STD Hotline
1–800–227–8922

ORGANIZATIONS

Church Mutual Insurance Company
3000 Schuster Lane
Merrill, Wisconsin 54452
> *Safety Tips on a Sensitive Subject: Child Sexual Abuse* is one of a series of protection booklets printed by this company. It is geared especially for churches and Christian ministries.

Department of Social Services or
Child Protection Services
> These governmental agencies will provide excellent pamphlets (often free of charge) from the U.S. Department of Health and Human Services and your state's Department of Social Services. These are succinct tools that can be used in various training settings and made available to everyone at your literature table.

Local Council on Child Abuse and Neglect
> Many communities have such a council that can provide literature, reading lists, and referrals for counseling.

Local Library
An array of titles will be available in many communities. Because understanding of the subject is increasing yearly, books with the most recent copyright will be the most reliable.

CHRISTIAN RESOURCES

BOOKS

Helping Victims of Sexual Abuse, by Lynn Heitritter and Jeanette Vought. Bethany House Publishers, Minneapolis: 1989.
This book covers diagnosis, treatment, and prevention. It is written from a Christian perspective to help counselors, victims, and families.

Victim Services Resource Manual: For pastors and lay leaders.
Child Protection Program Foundation
7441 Marvin D. Love Freeway
Suite 200
Dallas, Texas 75237
This manual lists an array of both religious and secular organizations with a brief description of what is available from each.

ORGANIZATIONS

Institute for Biblical Counseling
16075 West Belleview Avenue
Morrison, Colorado 80465
1–303–697–5425

IBC offers a three-day basic training seminar on sexual abuse. Advanced seminars dealing with recovery for men and recovery for women are also offered. They have a list of approved counselors across the nation for phone referrals.